BORDERLAND
in Butternut & Blue
A SAMPLER QUILT TO RECALL THE CIVIL WAR ALONG THE KANSAS/MISSOURI BORDER

Author: Barbara Brackman
Editor: Edie McGinnis
Technical Editor: Jane Miller
Designer: Kelly Ludwig, Ludwig Design, Inc.
Photography: Aaron T. Leimkuehler
Illustration: Lon Eric Craven
Production assistance: Jo Ann Groves

Published by:
Kansas City Star Books
1729 Grand Blvd.
Kansas City, Missouri, USA 64108

First edition, first printing
ISBN 978-1-933466-37-8

Printed in the United States of America by Walsworth
Publishing Co., Marceline, MO

To order copies, call StarInfo at (816) 234-4636 and
say "Books."

 KANSAS CITY STAR BOOKS

The Quilter's Home Page
www.PickleDish.com

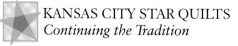 KANSAS CITY STAR QUILTS
Continuing the Tradition

ABOUT THE AUTHOR

Barbara Brackman has been writing about history since the 1970s. She grew up in Johnson County Kansas, and moved to Lawrence when she went to college at the University of Kansas. The Victorian town with its Civil War history captured her heart and she has lived there (with a few big city breaks) ever since.

Quilt history is her profession and local history is another passion. She's served as consultant for several museum exhibits on both, written quite a few books on quilts, in particular about quilts and the Civil War. She was the local history consultant when Ang Lee filmed *Ride With the Devil* in Kansas City, his movie about the border war starring Tobey Maguire and Jewel.

For Star Books, she has written *Women of Design: Quilts in the Newspaper* and *Prairie Flower: A Year on the Plains*. She also designs reproduction fabrics for Moda®.

CREDITS

Thanks go to Doug Weaver, Manager of Book Publishing at *The Kansas City Star*, Aaron T. Leimkuehler, our photographer, Jo Ann Groves for her imaging skills, Kelly Ludwig for her creative book design, and my editor, Edie McGinnis. Thanks also to Jane Miller for her technical skills and Lon Eric Craven for his clear, concise illustrations.

Many thanks to staff and students at Prairie Point Quilts in Shawnee where I taught the classes in Butternut and Blue that became the 2007 *Star* block of the month feature and this book. Special thanks to the quilters who finished their samplers in time for photographs and to my friends who made and quilted the projects.

The book wouldn't have nearly as many historical photographs without the digital files from the Library of Congress and the archives of the State Historical Society of Missouri and the Kansas State Historical Society. The librarians at the Mid-continent Public Library in Independence, Missouri, the Kansas City Public Library and the Kansas State Historical Society have also helped a good deal. And Marian Franklin deserves much credit for her website featuring the letters of her family, the Watts-Hays families, an invaluable online local history resource.

TABLE OF CONTENTS

The tattered quilt purchased in Missouri is signed "Elizabeth A. ?? 1848."

Unknown soldier. Photo Courtesy of the Library of Congress.

"Let us epitomize history: The Civil War originated on, in and over Kansas."

JOHN SPEER, KANSAS NEWSPAPERMAN

BETWEEN THE 1854 opening of the Kansas Territory and the 1861 Battle at Fort Sumter, the borderlands between Kansas and Missouri fueled brushfires that would explode into the firestorm of Civil War. Fort Sumter was the first official battle in a war that lasted four years, ending when Confederate General Robert E. Lee surrendered to Union General Ulysses S. Grant on April 12, 1865, in Appomattox Courthouse, Virginia. The names of the battlefields from Southern Pennsylvania to Southern Georgia are now a form of familiar American poetry: Shiloh, Manassas, Gettysburg, and Chickamauga.

This book recalls the lesser known Civil War—the skirmishes on either side of the Kansas/Missouri state line where people suffered some of the worst civilian casualties. Missouri had more official battles than many states in the deep South. Here we also remember the war's prelude, six years of unofficial civil war known at the time as the Kansas Troubles or Bleeding Kansas.

The book uses quilt blocks to tell the story of the Civil War along the Missouri/Kansas border. Each block in the Borderland Sampler is dedicated to the memory of a woman who lived through the war on the western frontier. The color theme of butternut and blue refers to the uniforms worn by the men. Union blue, a dark navy blue, became the uniform of the Federal Army during the war. Southern Confederate regulars might have obtained the blue gray of formal Confederate cloth, but Missourians often dressed in what was called butternut, a golden brown shade, dyed with walnut, the color that came to define the rural Southern guerrilla fighter.

Above left: An unknown solider in Union blue. Above right: An unknown Confederate soldier. The photo is black and white; we assume his coat is gray, but it could just as likely be light blue or butternut.

Civil War Quilt: Border Wars *by Sherry L. Dicus,*
Overland Park, Kansas, 2004.
Sherry appliquéd red stars over the sash
intersections for a splash of color and some detail
outside the block. She divided the 7" border into a 3"
finished inner border and a 4" finished outer border.
She typed each woman's story and transferred the
information to fabric for the center of quilt's back.

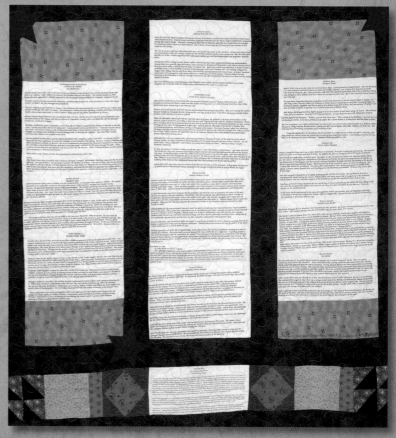

BORDERLAND: HISTORIC AND CULTURAL BACKGROUND

I've often thought that Delaware, small as it is, played a significant role in nineteenth-century American life as a buffer state, separating the slave state of Maryland from the free state of New Jersey. Out here, on the border between Missouri and Kansas, people could have used a buffer state. Yankees lived right by Southrons, Jayhawkers next to Border Ruffians and the cultural clash resounded through the land.

Missouri became a Southern state, a slave state, in 1821, even though most of it lay far above the Mason-Dixon line. Its central area along the Missouri River came to be known as Little Dixie while much of its western half remained wilderness even after the native tribes, the Osage, the Sac and the Fox had been forced west into Indian Territory.

White immigrants gradually populated the 24th state with a number of the pioneers being members of Daniel Boone's family. The old explorer came to the Missouri Territory, the story goes, because he thought Kentucky had grown too crowded. His children and grandchildren, Boones, Scholls and Hays, shared his fondness for unsettled country, creating a frontier culture in western Missouri, which they probably pronounced in Southern fashion ending in "uh" rather than "ee." But Missouri itself became crowded in a few decades according to Boone standards as more farmers came looking for land not yet worn out by decades of cultivation.

William Chick's memoirs recorded his parents leaving Alexandria, Virginia in the early spring of 1822, "for far-off Missouri."

"THEY TRAVELED IN LARGE FOUR-HORSE WAGONS TO CARRY THE HOUSEHOLD GOODS AND SERVANTS, AND WITH WHAT WAS THEN KNOWN AS A 'CARRY-ALL' FOR THE FAMILY…. IT WAS A LONG TRIP OVER THE ALLEGHENY MOUNTAINS OF NEARLY A MONTH'S TRAVEL TO FORT DUQUESNE, NOW KNOWN AS PITTSBURGH, PENNSYLVANIA. THEY CAMPED AT NIGHT, OR WHEN POSSIBLE LODGED IN SOME FARM HOUSE OR TAVERN, AS HOTELS WERE THEN KNOWN."

At the Ohio River they loaded their goods—slaves and hatboxes, horses and wagons—onto flatboats that transported them west to Shawneetown, Illinois. There they reloaded the wagons and bumped along by land to St. Louis, then through Missouri to Glasgow, north of Boonville.

In 1836, Chick's father "became restless on the farm" and moved the family to Westport, a town of about fifty people. The Chicks opened a store east of the corner where Kelly's Westport Tavern is today and prospered in what was to become Kansas City.

Western Missourians developed a society modeled on their former lives. Septimus Scholl had caught "the Missouri fever" with his Boone cousins and bought a hundred acres close to Independence, "in a neighborhood of respectable Kentuckian society which…pleases the old lady and Eliza (his wife and daughter)…they have become perfectly reconciled to spend their remaining days with [them]."

Women like Eliza and Sarah Scholl found comfort in churches, schools and sewing societies. Charles

Joseph LaTrobe, traveling through the hills of Jackson County, found signs of civilization in the early 1830s.

> "WE HEARD BY THE BARKING OF THE DOGS AND THE CHATTERING OF MANY VOICES, THAT WERE APPROACHING [A] FARM. [THE SETTLER] INFORMED US THAT HIS WIFE HAD GOT A NUMBER OF HER NEIGHBOURS WITH HER FOR A 'QUILTING FROLIC,' AND MADE US HEARTILY WELCOME. THE INTERIOR OF THE LOG HUT PRESENTED A SINGULAR SCENE. A SQUARE TABLE WAS SEEN TO OCCUPY A GREAT PART OF ITS FLOOR. IT WAS SURROUNDED BY A COMPACT BODY OF FEMALES, WHOSE FINGERS WERE OCCUPIED WITH ALL DILIGENCE UPON THE QUILT."

"Seppy" Scholl was cautious about his prospects. "This country is very singular from any that I ever saw. The land and climate are subject to the most sudden changes imaginable. The face of the country is generally poor, extensive prairie surrounded with small brush and large scrubby timber....If I had a big pile I would first invest it in the best land in Kentucky, second in Tennessee, third in Missouri."

Indigo calico prints atop a homespun Kentucky quilt.

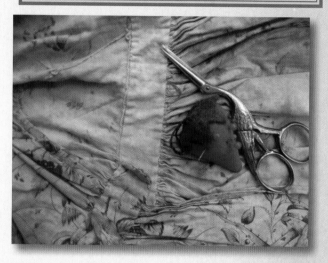

Reproduction sewing tools atop a hand-stitched baby dress from the early nineteenth century.

Yet the land had potential and was full of game. Scholl closed his letter: "We have killed several deer since we got here and a plenty more in the brush." Years later former slave Betty Brown recalled her mother's skill with her gun and traps. "My mama could hunt good as any man. Used to be a couple of peddler men come around with their packs. My mammy'd always have a pile of hides to trade with them for calico prints and trinkets, and such-like, but mostly for calico prints. She'd have coon hides and deer and mink and beaver."

"WE ARE TRAVELING THROUGH A POOR HILLY PART OF THE STATE WITH THE ROUGHEST, MOST GROTESQUE, LOOKING SET OF RUFFIAN SETTLERS IMAGINABLE. WHAT WOULD EASTERN VIRGINIANS THINK OF MEN BEING DRESSED IN BLUE COATS, RED STRIPED LINSEY WOOLSEY PANTS OR ELSE BLUE GEANES, PANTS AS WELL AS COATS, PINKS SHIRTS, RED CRAVATS AND PLAID VESTS? IT IS NO EXAGGERATION WHEN I SAY WE HAVE SEEN MANY SUCH IN THE LAST TWO DAYS. THE WOMEN ABOUT AS TASTILY DRESSED."
MARTHA J. WOOD. BOLLINGER COUNTY, MISSOURI, 1857.

People living in slavery made up a good percentage of Missouri's population. The 1860 census counted almost 4,000 slaves in Jackson County, 17% of its residents. Only 52 free blacks lived in the county. The counties with the greatest number of slaves were south of the Missouri River in Little Dixie and in the boot heel by the Mississippi River.

Missouri never had plantation systems for rice and cotton as in the deep south, but the land along its major rivers was a good place to grow hemp for the rope to bind those bales of cotton. Slave labor was an important asset in growing hemp and in turning the plant into rope. The stalks had to be retted and broken like linen, difficult and tiring work, and then the fibers twisted on what was called a rope walk. Slaves were also important in tobacco production but most Missouri slaveholders kept only a few people for their farm and domestic work. Slave owners often wrote of hiring their bondsmen out to others for extra cash.

In the 1930s, Harriet Lee told interviewers for the federal Works Progress Administration (WPA) oral history project about her mother who'd lived in slavery in eastern Missouri. "She never worked in the field, and she didn't know anything about cooking, but she did fine sewing. When they put her on the block they had some of her work there to show what fine sewing she could do. You know all the sewing was done by hand and my mammy'd sew sometimes till her fingers nearly dropped off. She sewed the finest tucks and she made all the fine tuck bosom shirts for the men."

Letha Taylor Meeks was a slave in Benton County near Warsaw and remembered the slave holders' "fine big house, we call it the mansion. They had porches and galleries. There were trees all around, pine trees and cedars, and oak trees. And the yard was full of flower bushes—big snowballs and lilacs, and rows of flags, and honeysuckle vines, with the mocking birds and doves as singing round—and there were jay birds too. And there were big vegetable gardens and fruit trees. In the store room in the fall there were always bags full of dried apples and peaches, and pumpkin and strings of onion a hanging up, and heaps of turnips and sweet taters, and bins full of taters."

By the 1850s, western Missouri had become an established Southern outpost. Ladies' academies in Independence and Lexington attracted students like Eliza Scholl and teachers like Mattie Livingston. Brick and stone buildings replaced the log huts of frontier days.

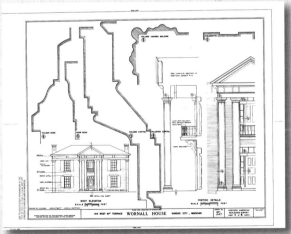

Kansas City's Wornall House still stands. This drawing by G. Engel is part of the Historic American Buildings Survey. Illustration courtesy of the Library of Congress.

Star quilt, unknown maker, estimated date: 1840-1860. Purchased in Missouri.

Missouri's greatest asset was its rivers. The Mississippi and the Missouri created a hub for western travel. The 1849 California Gold Rush brought thousands of men to Independence and Westport where they bought horses, wagons and shovels before heading into the Indian Territory along the road to California.

Commercial traffic on the Santa Fe Trail was a seasonal windfall to the Chicks, the Boones, the Hays and other Westport traders. In 1843 farmer Samuel Ralston wrote his wife: "From here started this summer to Santafee and Chihuahua 1500 waggons loaded with merchandize…It is the most singular—the most romantic and the most dangerous trade that is followed on the face of the globe."

Americans who traveled the California and Santa Fe trails came to covet the prairie. The land we call Kansas had long been home to Native Americans, nomadic tribes like the Kaw, the Pawnee and the Wichita. Missouri tribes and those removed from the Eastern states, such as the Delaware, Wyandot and Shawnee, had been promised perpetual reservations but Americans saw Indian Territory as empty space begging for white settlement and "civilization." In 1846 Edwin Bryant, a member of the Donner/Reed party on the trail to California, wrote:

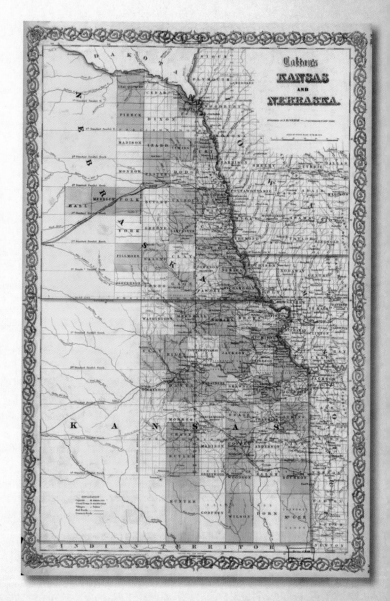

Stephen Douglas by the Brady studio, about 1860. Photograph Courtesy of the Library of Congress. Kansas' first Legislature named Douglas County, Kansas, after the man who conceived the Kansas-Nebraska Act.

The federal government permitted few whites to live in Kansas. Exceptions included Indian agents and traders, missionaries like Thomas and Sarah Johnson at the Shawnee Methodist Mission, and whites married to Native Americans, such as the husband of Nancy Quindaro Brown, part Wyandot and part Shawnee. These pioneer Kansans were positioned to benefit financially from land claims in the new Territory. Few gave any thought to the rights of the Native Americans who lived on the plains.

In 1854, Congress passed the Kansas-Nebraska Act to establish two new territories. Settlers would choose whether each would be slave state or free, an idea that seemed a practical compromise, an exercise in American democracy. The Kansas-Nebraska Act, however, has been called the "worst Pandora's box in our history." Opening the Kansas Territory released a cloud of troubles.

The bill's sponsor, Illinois Senator Stephen A. Douglas, hoped his concept of "popular sovereignty" would please both North and South and boost him into the Presidency. But the bill shocked many Northerners who believed slavery north of Arkansas had long ago been banned by a law called the Missouri Compromise. Many who had never given slavery much thought began to wonder about its future. Those who'd been in favor of abolishing slavery, reformers called abolitionists, grew indignant. Northerners, worried that Southern settlers would sway territorial elections, decided to move to Kansas.

> WE WENT TO BED ONE NIGHT, OLD-FASHIONED CONSERVATIVE, COMPROMISE, UNION WHIGS AND WAKED UP STARK MAD ABOLITIONISTS.
> AMOS LAWRENCE - JUNE 1854

In Ohio, Thomas and Matilda Barber prepared to emigrate with friends and relatives. The land boom was over in western Ohio but they might do well in Kansas while doing good for the free state cause. In Vermont, editors George and Clarina Nichols realized the struggle would be a war of words and made plans to move, joining numerous other journalists like Ohio's John Speer who packed his young family and a press. In Illinois, former Congressman Abraham Lincoln, whose political career seemed spent, was stirred enough to begin making speeches again, shaping a position on free territories that would lead him rather than Douglas to the Presidency.

In Kentucky, farmers like William and Mahala Doyle, who were working marginal lands, hoped for prosperity on the grassy plains. Missourians were the majority of the immigrants not only because they were closest, but because slaveholders like Henry Younger had the most to lose if Kansas became a free state. Missouri's

Senator David Atchison, running for re-election, realized that sectional rivalry made an excellent campaign issue. Only a month after the Kansas-Nebraska Act passed, he began giving fiery speeches, promising to terrorize any free-soil advocates who dared move to Kansas.

"[I] ADVISED IN A PUBLIC SPEECH…THE PEOPLE OF MISSOURI…HANG A NEGRO THIEF OR ABOLITIONIST, WITHOUT JUDGE OR JURY. THIS SENTIMENT MET WITH ALMOST UNIVERSAL APPLAUSE. ..WE WILL BEFORE SIX MONTHS ROLLS ROUND, HAVE THE DEVIL TO PAY IN KANSAS. . . . WE WILL BE COMPELLED, TO SHOOT, BURN & HANG, BUT THE THING WILL BE SOON OVER." LETTER FROM DAVID ATCHISON TO JEFFERSON DAVIS. SEPTEMBER 24, 1854.

Kansas settlers about 1855. Photo courtesy of the Kansas State Historical Society.

In Harrisonville Henry Younger drew papers for a proslavery settlement called Louisiana, Kansas Territory. Although he never actually lived there, he won election to the first Kansas Territorial Legislature from its district.

Kansas towns grew into free-state or proslavery camps. Atchison and Tecumseh were settled by southerner sympathizers while Osawatomie and Topeka were known as abolitionist strongholds. In free-state towns like Quindaro or Lawrence, a slave escaping from Missouri could find help in traveling to Canada. The network of antislavery partisans dedicated to freeing people by disobeying the law of the land was known as the Underground Railroad.

Missourians traveling to Kansas to vote, a free-state view. Kansas newcomers, hoping to elect like-minded legislators in the first elections, were stunned to find polling places overrun by Missourians who stuffed the ballot boxes.

"A NEGRO BELONGING TO MR. YOCUM… WAS RUN OFF AND HARBORED IN THE TOWN OF LAWRENCE….THE SCUM OF THE POPULATION OF THE EASTERN STATES, WHO ARE ENDEAVORING TO MONOPOLISE THIS TERRITORY, HAVE COMMENCED THEIR NEFARIOUS PRACTICES… IN A FEW MONTHS WE WILL SEE A REGULAR ORGANIZED "UNDERGROUND RAILROAD" IN KANSAS." ATCHISON SQUATTER SOVEREIGN, APRIL 10, 1855.

Small militia armies were common. The proslavery Kansas Militia was composed primarily of Missourians, the Bloomington Guards and the Prairie City Boys were antislavery. Dozens of groups practiced marching and drilling, armed with pistols, knives and the efficient new rifled guns known as Sharpe's Rifles. Name calling and threats turned to beatings and then murder as a widening circle of terrorism and revenge earned the territory the name Bleeding Kansas. Kansas became a magnet for partisans on both sides, among them John Brown, a militant New York abolitionist. While visiting his sons, he led a murderous attack on three members of the Doyle family and two other neighbors in the 1856 Pottawatomie Massacre.

> "MY HUSBAND TOLD ME TO GO TO A NEIGHBOR WHO LIVED ABOUT A QUARTER OF A MILE AWAY AND TELL HIM THE BORDER-RUFFIANS, AS WE CALLED THEM, WERE COMING—I PICKED UP MY BABY AND RAN ALL THE WAY OVER THERE…. A MAN JUST RIDING AROUND THE CORNER OF THE HOUSE SAID, 'ALL MISSOURI IS COMING OVER HERE TO DRIVE THE DAMNED YANKEES OUT.'" ELIZABETH STORRS RECALLING A RAID ON HER FARM IN DOUGLAS COUNTY, MAY 26, 1856.

In 1857, the Kansas Troubles cooled as many proslavery partisans left the Territory, realizing their cause was lost. But explosions of border brutality continued until the end of the national Civil War in 1865. The border war that began as militia units battling over political differences deteriorated into raiding troops of bandits, nicknamed "freebooters" or "jayhawks" on the Kansas side, "border ruffians," "bushwhackers" or "butternuts" on the Missouri side.

Missouri Town. Split rail fences had many nicknames including worm fence or Virginia fence, indicating a regional style.

Alfred R. Waud sketched a guerrilla soldier during the Civil War. Illustration courtesy of the Library of Congress.

A GLOSSARY OF NICKNAMES AND INSULTS

Black Republican – In the South after 1856, any free-state sympathizer or anti-slavery advocate but particularly members of the Republican party, assumed to be empathetic to African-Americans

Bluestocking – An educated or literate woman

Border Ruffian or Ruffian – An uncouth Missourian using force to advocate a proslavery Kansas. During the War, slang for pro-Confederate guerrilla fighters

Bushwhacker – Synonymous with Border Ruffian

Butternut – A poor Southerner wearing rough clothing. During the War, slang for any uncouth Confederate soldier or sympathizer.

Contraband – During the War, slang for a former slave generally one sticking close to the Union Armies

Copperhead – During the War, a "venomous biped of Northern birth and Southern sympathies," according to *Bartlett's Dictionary of Americanisms*.

Doughface – A Northern politician with Southern sympathies, particularly before the War

Freebooter – A soldier of fortune without official government sanction

Jayhawker or Jayhawk - An uncouth Kansan using force to advocate a free Kansas. During the War, slang for rampaging Union troops

Pike or Piker – A tramp, a poor Missourian, one who did not pay his debts

Puke – An indelicate nickname for an uncouth Missourian

Red Leg – During the War, synonymous with Jayhawker along the Missouri-Kansas border

Secesh – During the War, a Confederate soldier or sympathizer

Southron – A term used in the South to describe a Southerner

Yankee or Damned Yankee – A term used North and South to describe a Northerner, damned only in the South

Politics separated people along the border but cultural differences added fuel to the fire. The invisible line between Kansas and Missouri also separated northeastern and southern cultures. Every place Southerners and Northerners lived side by side we find people remarking on their neighbors' ways. Visitors such as Georgia college boys at Princeton or Yale, plantation owners spending summer vacations in New England or Northern governesses in Southern mansions often wrote home about food, clothing, language and attitudes. Most found the differences amusing and most found their own folkways superior as did Sophie Chopin, a Vermonter living in the South. "I wish you could see the way they do things here sometimes and expect you would laugh as much as I do....They are far behind New England.... "

Amusement was too often colored by prejudice. A Mormon traveler through rural Missouri in 1831 wrote:

"THE INHABITANTS ARE EMIGRANTS FROM TENNESSEE, KENTUCKY, VIRGINIA, AND THE CAROLINAS, ETC. WITH CUSTOMS, MANNERS, MODES OF LIVING AND A CLIMATE ENTIRELY DIFFERENT FROM THE NORTHERNERS, AND THEY HATE YANKEES WORSE THAN SNAKES, BECAUSE THEY HAVE CHEATED THEM OR SPECULATED ON THEIR CREDULITY, WITH SO MANY CONNECTICUT WOODEN CLOCKS AND NEW ENGLAND NOTIONS."

With so much politically at stake, hostility intensified along the Kansas-Missouri border and into the Civil War. In 1863, a Union soldier described Missouri: "said to be a God-forsaken country....One who draws conclusions from the general appearance of the genuine Butternuts is apt to believe that Providence has not been over lavish in favors towards the Pukes."

Pukes and Pikes were common nicknames for Missourians in the decades before the Civil War when Ohioans were called Buckeyes, Kentuckians Corncrackers, Indianans Hoosiers and Illinois settlers were known as Suckers. Like most slang, nickname origins are impossible to pin down and stories abound. Pike or Piker is generally attributed to the California Gold Rush days when so many Missourians from Pike County tried their luck in the west and wound up broke and in debt. In 1854, Illinois' former Governor Thomas Ford wrote that "sucker" and "puke" originated in Illinois' lead mining culture of the 1820s. A sucker was a poor Southern immigrant who'd been stripped from the wealthier plantation society the way tobacco farmers strip suckers or wayward roots from the plant. Missouri puked out its own poor lead miners. "By the names of Suckers and Pukes Illinoisans and Missourians are likely to be called, amongst the vulgar forever."

Differences between Kansans and Missourians extended to subtleties of architecture and religion.

Southerners thought no better of Yankees, a word that had its own air of vulgarity. New Englanders were derided as Brother Jonathan and any Northerner might be insulted as a "Black Republican" or a "Black Abolitionist." "Oh! Those long-faced, sanctimonious psalm singing Yankees," complained an Atchison newspaper editor.

Beyond insults, culture shaped daily lives and bigotry. In 1785, Southerner Thomas Jefferson characterized Northerners as cool, sober, and industrious yet full of chicanery and hypocrisy. "In the South they are fiery, voluptuary, indolent [yet] candid and generous."

Foodways often scandalized travelers. In 1835, Northerner Lucy Maynard wrote about her Illinois neighbors' opinion of her New England boiled dinner. "They think that a boiled dish as we boil it is not fit to eat; it is true they boil their food but each separate...I speak of it because it is so different."

Southerners tended to cook spicier, fattier food served in courses. They grew corn for grits and mush, cornbread and whiskey. New Englanders liked what was called "light bread" made from wheat or brown bread made from rye and other grains. They were fond of what we might call one-dish casseroles, legumes cooked into pease porridge or baked beans. Their diet relied on what were called Irish potatoes. Southerners ate sweet potatoes and looked to pork for protein. While Southerners cooked over open fireplaces, Yankees considered an iron stove a frontier necessity.

Northerners liked coffee and tea; Southerners drank buttermilk, water sweetened with molasses and many enjoyed a "daily constitutional" of sugar and whiskey for breakfast. Northerners drank hard cider if they drank spirits. Many Kansas newcomers were members of temperance organizations who refrained from alcoholic beverages and aimed to persuade their neighbors to do the same.

A Successful Skirmish at Independence.
Kansas City, Wednesday, Feb. 26.

A skirmish occurred at Independence on the 16th, between a detachment of Ohio Cavalry and a band of rebels headed by Quantel Parker. The latter were routed, with a loss of three killed, several wounded and several taken prisoners. A quantity of arms were also captured. The National loss was one killed and three wounded.

An 1862 bulletin from the New York Times. William Quantrill was earning a national reputation but it was years before his actual name and identity were pinned down.

The Confederate Memorial in the cemetery at Troost and Gregory.

Speech also defined an immigrant's origins. New Englanders spoke rapidly in a high pitch; Southerners stretched out their vowels. Southerners "reckoned", while Northerners "guessed". Yankees carried a pail to milk a "ke-ow"; Missourians toted a bucket to milk a cow. Pronunciation and dialect was so markedly different that settlers could easily identify friends and enemies. Just weeks after President Franklin Pierce signed the Kansas-Nebraska Act an Indiana newspaper reported from the Territory:

"THOUSANDS AND THOUSANDS ARE POURING IN FROM ALL PORTIONS OF THE UNION, BUT MORE ESPECIALLY FROM MISSOURI, KENTUCKY AND TENNESSEE….THERE IS A STORY ABROAD THAT AT ALL THE FERRIES OVER THE MISSOURI RIVER THEY HAVE A COW TIED, AND A COMMITTEE TO WATCH ALL IMMIGRANTS. THE COMMITTEE ASK OF EACH IMMIGRANT WHAT ANIMAL THAT IS? IF HE SAYS "A COW', ALL WELL---HE GOES OVER. BUT IF HE ANSWERS 'A KEOW' THEY TURN HIM BACK.

This story is probably myth, a legend told about discordant cultures that goes back generations, but like many myths, it reflects truths. Speech ways were different and the factions were hostile from the very beginning of territorial settlement. Another truth: Newspapers fanned the flames. "Bleeding Kansas" made excellent copy.

MISSOURI 1860

115,000 people lived in slavery in Missouri in 1860.

Slaves between 25% and 37% of the population

Slaves between 15% and 24% of population

BUTTERNUT AND BLUE: CHOOSING FABRIC

THE BORDERLAND SAMPLER focuses on shades of blue and brown. The colors echo dyes found in Civil War era quilts, but they also symbolize the conflict on the Kansas/Missouri border. Our American memory may recall the Civil War in shades of Union blue and Confederate gray but the western war was fought in Yankee blue and butternut brown.

During the 1930s, interviewers with the federal Works Progress Administration (WPA) talked to many who had lived in slavery. Rachel Goings of Cape Girardeau, Missouri, remembered the soldiers seventy years earlier: "We could always tell them. The rebels wore brown coats and the Northerners wore blue suits with pretty gold pieces on their shoulders."

Tishy Taylor had a similar memory of the Blue Coats and the Brown Coats but the interviewer who typed his comments replaced the word brown with gray in parentheses. Taylor accurately remembered his own Missouri history but the interviewer's Civil War was colored in nostalgic blue and gray.

The men Taylor called Blue Coats wore Union blue uniforms of factory-woven woolen fabric, probably dyed with indigo or Prussian blue, the two most common blue coloring agents at the time. The Yankee uniform was consistent because the Union had factories for cloth and clothing production, access to wool and to imported dyes.

Gray cloth for Confederate uniforms was a luxury for foot soldiers particularly in the West. Even well-to-do officers had a hard time obtaining uniform fabric. Mississippian Tryphena Fox wrote about a trade her physician husband negotiated with a patient, "She made him a beautiful piece of gray homespun jeans. It is as fine and pretty as boughtten goods...Now he looks quite genteel as well as Confederate."

With little access to imported dyes and manufactured cloth, the rural Southern uniform was diverse. A woman in Ohio wrote of seeing "a great many Rebel prisoners of war ...a motley set, dressed in garments of every conceivable style, material and color, yellow, red, blue, gray, butternut, etc. Around some, dirty old bed quilts were thrown..."

Many Confederates relied on an unofficial uniform of home-dyed cloth colored with walnut hulls and bark, fabric called butternut. The White Walnut tree (*Juglans cinerea*), nicknamed the butternut tree, dyes fibers a variety of browns from tan to dark. Butternut trees grow throughout the eastern United States, thriving in southern and central Missouri. West of Boonville the Black Walnut provides similar dyes.

A dish of black walnuts atop a quilt made about 1850. The backing is the golden brown typical of cotton dyed with the husks and bark of Black Walnut trees or White Walnuts, nicknamed Butternuts.

Northerners with Southern sympathies were also called Copperheads during the Civil War. Some wore jewelry made of a Liberty-head copper penny—a copperhead. I found this "large cent" drilled with a hole in an Indiana family's estate. Did someone once wear this penny around her neck to convey her secret loyalties?

Butternut is a golden brown ranging from light to dark and rather bright to very drab. We see a similar shade of brown jeans fabric in Carhartt work clothing worn today. Butternut was more than a color, however, it became a symbol. Before the Civil War, the term was used to describe a Southern rural person dressed in simple homespun clothing. During the War the word came to mean Southern partisans whether Confederate soldier or secret Southern sympathizer.

Northerners with Confederate loyalties might wear jewelry made from butternuts to identify themselves. An Indiana Unionist remembered seeing "many butternut pins, the emblem worn by disloyal women." A cut walnut shell could be viewed as a pair of hearts, representing both the Northern and the Southern heart.

CHOOSING REPRODUCTION FABRICS

Each of the blocks in the sampler features dark, medium and light contrast. You can buy quarter yard pieces for a scrappy style. If you prefer a more coordinated look buy yard sized pieces of a few fabrics – 3 butternuts, 2 blues and 2 contrasts.

You'll need butternuts in light, medium and dark and some blues in medium and dark. For contrast, try tans or ivories for the light areas and dark browns for the darks. You can also add red or a true yellow for a livelier look.

Think about prints of various sizes to get the chintz look that was popular in the Civil War era. Or you might want to focus on wovens—plaids, stripes and checks. Wovens were the fabric of everyday work clothes for men and women and would give the quilt the simple look you'd find on the frontier in 1860.

BUTTERNUTS:

In reproductions—look for prints, plaids or plains in golden browns. For a true butternut look avoid reddish browns and very dark browns – although these two shades offer a nice contrast to the butternut gold.

BLUES:

For Yankee blues, look for what we call navy blue, a dark neutral blue with no purple or greenish tints, the color of the field in the American flag.

SETTING OPTIONS FOR THE SAMPLERS

At the end of the book on page 114 you'll find instructions for various setting options. Look there for yardage information.

PATTERN MEASUREMENTS

Any pieced sampler presents problems in basic geometry. The blocks here are based on 14" and some are based on four sections; others on three.

Mathematical problems are easily solved with BlockBase and Electric Quilt (EQ6), the computer programs used to draft the patterns. The programs calculate cutting instructions when the numbers do not work out evenly. For example, dividing 14 by 3 results in Nine-Patch squares finishing to 4 2/3", which the computer program might round down to 4 5/8". When pieced together with extreme accuracy the block finishes to 13 7/8", an eighth of an inch short.

Do not worry about this. You can easily adjust for the 1/16-inch difference on either side when you are setting the block.

QUILTS & PROJECTS

Borderland Sampler made by Jeanne Poore, Overland Park, Kansas 2005. Quilted by Fabric Arts.

BLOCK 1

NORTH STAR

FOR MRS. HENRY CLAY BRUCE A RUNAWAY SLAVE

14" Finished Block

THE NORTH STAR BLOCK WAS MADE BY JEANNE POORE OF OVERLAND PARK, KANSAS.

THE CONFLICT BETWEEN North and South was based on slavery, an economic system brought to Missouri by Southerners who settled the state. We can catch a glimpse of the slaves' lives here because a few, like Henry Clay Bruce, wrote their memories.

Bruce lived as a slave in north-central Missouri until March 30, 1864. Although the Emancipation Proclamation had been in effect for over a year by that date, nothing had changed for Bruce and his African-American neighbors in Linn and Chariton Counties. He was courting a young woman belonging to a man named Farmer who banned him from the property. A slave like

Henry, who could read the newspapers and tell others of the freedom promised by Lincoln's Emancipation Proclamation, was a threat.

In his autobiography, Henry didn't mention Miss Farmer's first name, but he told the story of how the frustrated lovers decided to elope and escape to the free state of Kansas. One night they met on a secluded road. She had "her worldly effects tied up in a handkerchief and I took her up on the horse behind me...We avoided the main road and reached Laclede in safety, where we took the train for St. Joe, thence to Weston, where we crossed the Missouri River on a ferry boat to Fort Leavenworth, Kansas."

Above: In 1863, Alfred R. Waud sketched a group of refugees from slavery. Illustration courtesy of the Library of Congress.

ENRY AND BLANCHE Bruce might have spent their youths in freedom had their mother been aware of the workings of the Underground Railroad. When Henry was about six, his owner took the boys and their mother from his Missouri farm back to Virginia. While on a boat steaming east on the Ohio River between the slave state of Kentucky and the free state of Ohio, well-meaning white passengers informed the slaves that when the boat landed at Cincinnati, abolitionists would take them away. The women, ignorant of their rights in a free state, were frightened enough by the offer to inform their master of the plan. He arranged to drop his property off in Kentucky and avoid Ohio altogether. Their naiveté, Henry recalled, caused him to work as a slave for seventeen more years.

To learn more about the Bruces, Missouri slaves who became a prominent American family, read:
Henry Clay Bruce, *The New Man: Twenty-Nine Years a Slave, Twenty-Nine Years a Free Man*. Originally printed in 1895; reprint Negro Universities Press, 1969.
Lawrence Otis Graham, *The Senator and the Socialite: The True Story of America's First Black Dynasty*. Harper Collins, 2006.

Henry Clay Bruce as pictured in his autobiography.

MR. AND MRS. RAY'S MISSION IN KANSAS CITY, MISSOURI

Both Henry and Blanche Bruce founded schools offering African-Americans a first step up from slavery. Private schools offered the only access to education for many. Lloyd and Emma Ray founded this school and mission in Kansas City about 1900.

Like many other escapees, they traveled at night pursued by irate owners. Because Henry knew the local roads well, he didn't have to keep an eye on the North Star, the traditional navigational tool for the runaway. This couple's journey took them west. Once across the Missouri the runaways were free. They married and lived in Leavenworth and Atchison. The 1880 census found Henry, his two daughters and two sons living without her. We can assume she died about that time.

Henry's brother, Blanche K. Bruce, also escaped from slavery into Kansas. Henry and his children accompanied Blanche to Washington where Blanche was elected a Senator from Mississippi, our first elected African-American senator to serve a full term.

Several traditional patchwork designs bear the name North Star. This one, a star crisscrossed by paths, was given the name by the Lockport Batting Company in the 1930s. The pattern recalls the Underground Railroad and Mrs. H. C. Bruce.

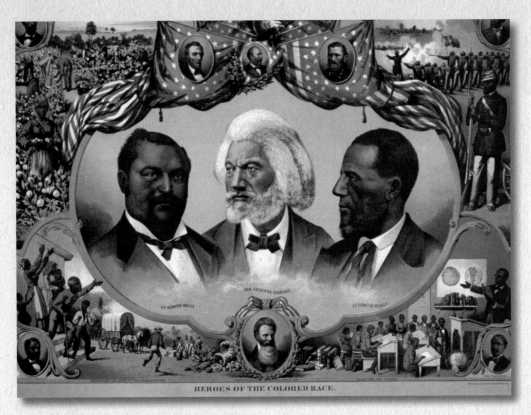

Henry Bruce's brother, Blanche Kelso Bruce, is portrayed on the left as one of the "Heroes of the Colored Race" in a lithograph printed in 1881. Frederick Douglass is in the center and Bruce's fellow Senator, Hiram Revels, is on the right. Photograph courtesy of the Library of Congress.

In 1936, Theodore LaVack photographed this hundred-year-old slave cabin on John O'Fallon's estate in eastern Missouri. Photograph courtesy of the Library of Congress' Historical American Buildings Survey.

ROTARY CUTTING

- ✪ Piece A - Cut 4 medium strips 8 1/8" by 2 1/8". Use the template to cut the angles.
- ✪ Piece B - Cut 4 dark squares 3 1/8". Cut each in half diagonally to make 8 triangles.
- ✪ Piece C - Cut 1 dark square 8 1/4". Cut twice on the diagonal to make 4 triangles.
- ✪ Piece D - Cut 4 light strips 5 3/4" by 2 1/8". Use the template to cut the angle. Reverse the template and cut 4 more light.
- ✪ Piece E - Cut 4 dark and 5 medium squares 2 1/8".

TO MAKE THE BLOCK

- ✪ This block is constructed on the diagonal. Sew the B triangles to the D and Dr strips. Stitch the strips you just made to either side of the A strips. You need to make four of these ABD units.

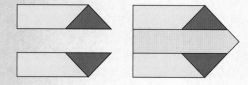

- ✪ Sew a dark C triangle to either side of an ABD unit. Make two sections like this. One will be the upper right portion of the block, the other will be the lower left portion.

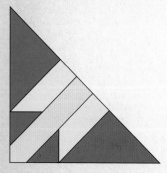

- ✪ The middle section of the block is made by sewing the E squares together. Alternate the dark and medium squares and make a nine-patch unit. Refer to the colored diagram for color placement. Sew an ABD unit to either side of the nine-patch.

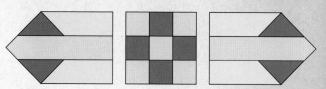

- ✪ Sew the three sections together to complete the block.

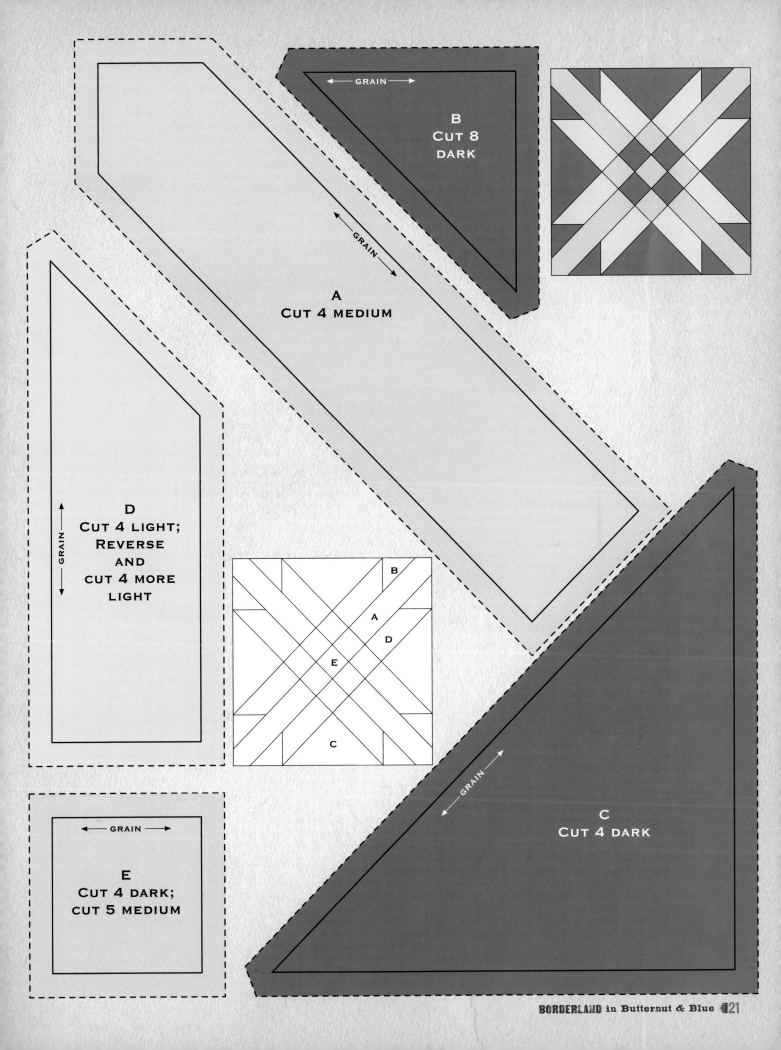

B
CUT 8
DARK

←GRAIN→

GRAIN

A
CUT 4 MEDIUM

D
CUT 4 LIGHT;
REVERSE
AND
CUT 4 MORE
LIGHT

GRAIN

B

A

D

E

C

GRAIN

C
CUT 4 DARK

←GRAIN→

E
CUT 4 DARK;
CUT 5 MEDIUM

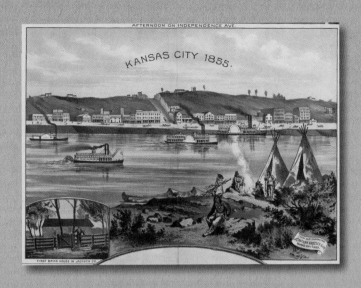

BLOCK 2
INDIAN PLUME

FOR WARPOLE'S DAUGHTER A WYANDOT

14" Finished Block

THE INDIAN PLUME BLOCK WAS MADE BY PAT MOORE OF KANSAS CITY, KANSAS.

AMERICAN INDIAN POLICY in the mid-nineteenth century assigned the Kansas City area as home for many of the tribes who'd been forced from Eastern lands. Among them were the Wyandot or Huron people, whose reserve was at the mouth of the Kansas River where it flowed into the Missouri, a good spot for trading, farming and hunting. Today we call the site Kansas City, Kansas.

One of the Wyandot leaders, called Warpole in English, had a daughter whose name wasn't recorded when a man from the States met her in 1857 at a cabin in the "Wyandot Forest." The woman was "of great size and stature....fully six

feet tall, and her toggery and appearance unusual and striking. Her garments were made of nicely tanned, soft, yellowish doeskins that resemble chamois, embroidered and loudly decorated with tassels, beads, ribbons, the plumage of birds, and with pearls, and silver, and gold...altogether gay and stunning....She scarcely condescended to notice me."

This woman might have been Catherine Warpole Whitewing whose name appears on an 1867 roll of Wyandots. The Wyandot people originated in what is now Canada, moved south into Ohio and then were forced on to Indiana and Kansas. Many began to cede their Kansas lands in 1855

Above: A nostalgic view of the city of Kansas viewed from the Wyandot's side of the river. Illustration courtesy of the Library of Congress.

and moved south to the border with Oklahoma, leaving their name on the county where their community once thrived.

Indian Plume was a pattern from Kansas City's Aunt Martha needlework company in the 1930s. The firm is still in the city, now called Colonial Patterns. You can see their sign near I-70 in downtown Kansas City, Missouri, not far from what was the Wyandot Reserve in the years before the Civil War.

The Huron Cemetery, just west of the public library in downtown Kansas City, Kansas, was preserved in the early twentieth century through the efforts of the Conley sisters, descendents of the Wyandot-Huron people who came to Kansas.

ROTARY CUTTING

- ✪ A – Cut the following squares 3 1/8". Cut each in half diagonally to make 2 triangles
  - ★ 3 dark squares to make 6 triangles
  - ★ 12 light to make 24 triangles
  - ★ 15 medium to make 30 triangles
- ✪ B – Cut 2 dark squares 2 7/8"
- ✪ C – Cut 1 dark square 5 1/8"
- ✪ Sew all rotary cut pieces using a scant quarter inch seam.

TO MAKE THE BLOCK

- ✪ Make 24 half-square triangles using light and medium A triangles.

- ✪ Make 6 half-square triangles using medium and dark A triangles.

- ✪ Sew the pieces together row by row. Sew the rows together to complete the block as shown.

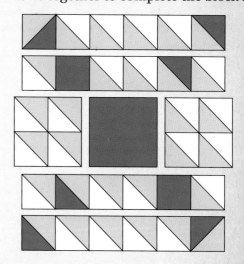

TEMPLATE FOR A
CUT 6 DARK,
24 LIGHT,
30 MEDIUM

TEMPLATE FOR SQUARE B
CUT 2 DARK

A

B

C

TEMPLATE FOR SQUARE C
CUT 1 DARK

BLOCK 3
SOUTHERN STAR

FOR SARAH DAVIS JOHNSON A MISSIONARY

14" Finished Block

THE SOUTHERN STAR BLOCK WAS MADE BY JEANNE POORE OF OVERLAND PARK, KANSAS.

SOUTHERN STAR IS an old design, first published in the magazine *Hearth & Home* about 1900. The block represents Sarah T. Davis Johnson (1810-1873) born in Bourbon County, Kentucky. She was the daughter of two Kentucky pioneers who spent their youth among the Shawnee after being captured in 1780, during the American Revolution.

Her mother was Sarah Ruddel whose family had come to Kentucky from Virginia about the same time as pioneer Daniel Boone or soon after. In 1780, when she was 17, British troops, in legion with the Shawnee, attacked their Kentucky settlement, killed several people and captured

dozens. The Shawnee took the captives to the Detroit area, where they lived as Shawnee for several years.

Upon their release in 1784, Sarah Ruddel married fellow captive Thomas Davis. The Davis family became early Missouri settlers in the Mississippi River town of Clarksville in Pike County, where the younger Sarah married Methodist minister Thomas Johnson in 1830. Their honeymoon journey took them to Indian Territory west of the Missouri state line. There they spent many years ministering to the Shawnee tribe, built the Shawnee Mission and developed the training school there.

Above: Sarah Davis Johnson. Photograph courtesy of the Kansas State Historical Society.

The Johnsons were among the earliest Kansas residents of European descent, yet Sarah Johnson was probably quite familiar with the Shawnee language and Shawnee culture. Her Uncle Stephen Ruddel or Ruddle, also a captive, was famous for having been raised with Shawnee leader, Tecumseh. He became a minister to the tribe after his release.

When the Methodist Church split into proslavery and antislavery factions, the Johnsons, who kept several slaves at the Mission, aligned themselves according to their Kentucky and Virginia heritage with the Southern Methodists. Thomas felt so strongly about the pro-slavery view that he ran for a seat in the Kansas Territorial Legislature in 1855, vowing to bring the new state into the Union as a slave state. Both he and son Alexander were elected to Kansas' first territorial government, an authority that free-state Kansans called the Bogus Legislature because it was elected primarily by Missourians who rode into Kansas to vote. Under Johnson, the Legislature met at the Shawnee Mission where they outlawed any speech and actions dedicated to freeing slaves.

Although they were soon replaced by a free-state government reflecting the views of the majority of actual Kansas settlers, the first Legislature left a legacy in the names they gave the new counties. An old poem rhymes: "Many a legislator's bid to fame is a county born to bear his name." Johnson County is Sarah's husband's memorial.

In 1858, the Johnsons retired to a home at 35th and Agnes. When the Civil War broke out, they were strong Unionists who tried to remain neutral in the guerrilla fighting that afflicted the Kansas City area. In the final winter of the War, Thomas Johnson answered a knock on his door one night. Men who asked for a drink of water shot him through the door as he closed it. He died in Sarah's arms. Like so many other murders at the time, Johnson's assassination was never solved. Some said Quantrill's Confederate guerrillas killed him in a botched robbery; others believed embittered Kansans had their final revenge for his proslavery politics.

Thomas and Sarah Johnson's memorial is in a small graveyard a few blocks from the Shawnee Mission.

VISIT

The Shawnee Indian Mission, a State Historic Site, at 3403 West 53rd Street in Fairway. The brick buildings have been restored to look much as they did in Sarah Johnson's time.

The Shawnee Mission Cemetery at 3201 Shawnee Mission Parkway in Fairway. The small cemetery, maintained as a State Historic Site, is between Chadwick and Canterbury on the south side of the highway. Park on a side street and walk to the gate. It's open daily.

Note the large memorial to Sarah Davis Johnson and her husband Thomas and also the grave of the elder Sarah Davis (1763-1865) who lived a long and extraordinary life. Sarah Ruddel Davis spent her later years at the Shawnee Mission where she presumably renewed old acquaintance with people she knew in her youth.

Above: The West building at the Shawnee Mission was built in 1837.

TO MAKE THE BLOCK

See the pattern pieces for the cutting directions.

✪ Sew each A piece to a B piece.

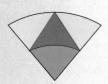

✪ Add a C piece to one side of A and a C reverse to the other.

✪ Sew a D piece to the left of each ABC unit.

✪ Sew all ABCD units together.

✪ Stitch the F pieces to the outer edge.

✪ Appliqué the E circle in place to complete the block

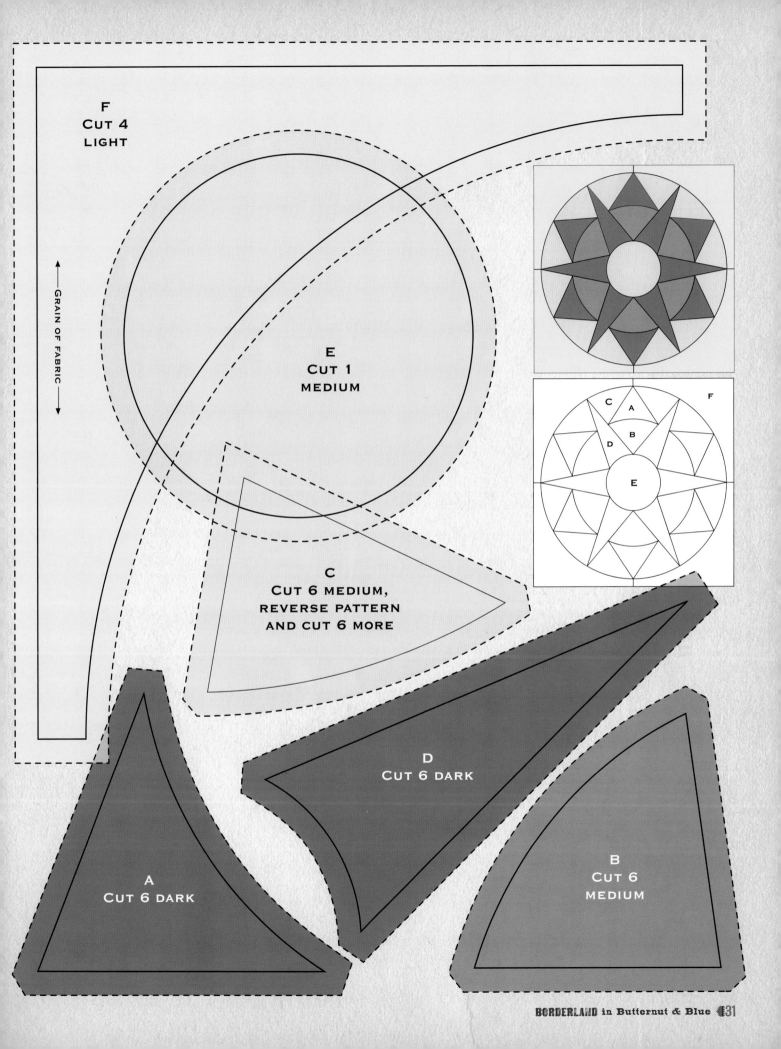

F
CUT 4
LIGHT

GRAIN OF FABRIC

E
CUT 1
MEDIUM

C
CUT 6 MEDIUM,
REVERSE PATTERN
AND CUT 6 MORE

D
CUT 6 DARK

A
CUT 6 DARK

B
CUT 6
MEDIUM

PROJECT 1

SOUTHERN STARS

BY DOROTHY LEBOEUF

Quilt 84" x 98" · 14" Block · 7" Borders

SOUTHERN STARS, HAND PIECED AND MACHINE QUILTED BY DOROTHY LEBOEUF, ROGERS, ARKANSAS, 2005, FROM THE COLLECTION OF DONALD AND IRMA JEAN BARTA.

FABRIC REQUIREMENTS

- ✪ 5/8 yard for piece E
- ✪ 4 yards for piece C
- ✪ 2 yards for piece A
- ✪ 1 3/4 yards for piece B
- ✪ 2 yards for piece D
- ✪ 3 1/4 yards for piece F
- ✪ 4 yards printed plaid or chintz scale floral for the border and binding

MAKE 30 SOUTHERN STAR BLOCKS

- ✪ See the pattern on page 31 for instructions on making the 30 circular stars.

CUTTING THE BORDERS

- ✪ Cut 2 strips of fabric 7 1/2" x 84 1/2" for the side borders
- ✪ Cut 2 strips of fabric 7 1/2" x 98 1/2" for the side borders

PIECING THE CIRCULAR STARS

- ✪ See the instructions on page 30.

SETTING THE QUILT

- ✪ Sew the blocks together in rows. There are five blocks across and 6 blocks down.
- ✪ Sew a 7 1/2" x 84 1/2" border to either side of the quilt. Add the remaining two borders to the top and bottom to complete the quilt top.

QUILTING

Dorothy added dimension to her piecing by machine quilting around each piece of the star right in the ditch (in the seam). She added a spiral to the circle in the center of the stars and a grid to the setting shapes. She created parallel lines of quilting in the busy border fabric.

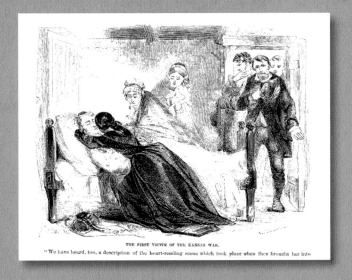

THE FIRST VICTIM OF THE KANSAS WAR.
"We have heard, too, a description of the heart-rending scene which took place when they brought her into

BLOCK 4

MEMORY WREATH

FOR MATILDA COSLEY BARBER
A NORTHERN WIDOW

14" Finished Block

THE MEMORY WREATH BLOCK WAS STITCHED BY PAT MOORE OF KANSAS CITY, KANSAS.

MATILDA BARBER CAN be viewed as the Civil War's first widow. Her husband, Thomas, was shot in December 1855, six years before the battle at Fort Sumter officially marked the official beginning of the conflict.

The Barbers came to the Kansas Territory from New Paris, Ohio, with family and neighbors who hoped to prosper and cast a vote for freedom in Kansas. The New Paris colony settled west of Lawrence. During their first year, hostilities developed between free-state settlers and Missouri immigrants who advocated slavery. In

November, a young man named Charles Dow was shot and killed near what is now Vinland in Douglas County. In December 1855, the county erupted with armed camps of free-state and proslavery militia fighting small battles in a week-long event known as the Wakarusa War. Thomas Barber was killed as he rode home from Lawrence to visit Tillie one morning. His murderers were a group of Missourians who'd formed a "Kansas Militia."

Tillie Barber's husband was the only casualty of the Wakarusa War. He became an antislavery

Above: "The First Victim of the Kansas War." An illustration from an 1855 book The War in Kansas: A Rough Trip to the Border.

martyr and Kansas a national cause when poet John Greenleaf Whittier memorialized his murder and Tillie's grief in *Burial of Barber*. Poetry had the power to capture the American imagination at the time and many a Northerner memorized the lines:

"Bear him, comrades, to his grave;
Never over one more brave
Shall the prairie grasses weep."

Thomas Barber's funeral was held at the Free State Hotel, which was burned a few months later by the same "Kansas Militia" blamed for his death. In 1867, Alexander Gardner photographed the rebuilt hotel known as the Eldridge House. Photograph Courtesy of the Library of Congress.

Tillie Barber also became a national symbol. "Words can never convey...the heart crushing agony of the young wife. There were no children in the household, and all the affection had twined around this one idol," wrote one mythmaker. She remained in Kansas, married again to N.C. Blood and raised a daughter, Katie.

A century and a half later, Thomas Barber's name is almost forgotten. Kansas has a Barber County. Douglas County has a historic site called the Barber School and Thomas' grave is marked with a large monument in Lawrence's Pioneer Cemetery. The Memory Wreath block was given its name by Carrie Hall, a Leavenworth seamstress who wrote a book about quilt patterns in 1935.

WHITTIER'S
BURIAL OF BARBER

BEAR HIM, COMRADES, TO HIS GRAVE;
NEVER OVER ONE MORE BRAVE
SHALL THE PRAIRIE GRASSES WEEP....

PLANT THE BUCKEYE ON HIS GRAVE
FOR THE HUNTER OF THE SLAVE
IN ITS SHADOW CANNOT REST;
AND LET MARTYR, MOUND AND TREE
BE OUR PLEDGE AND GUARANTY
OF THE FREEDOM OF THE WEST!"

ROTARY CUTTING

- ✪ A – Cut 4 light 4" squares.
- ✪ B – Cut the following squares 4 3/4". Cut each twice on the diagonal to make four triangles.
  - ★ Cut 2 light squares for 8 triangles
  - ★ Cut 2 medium light squares for 8 triangles.
  - ★ Cut 1 medium square for 4 triangles
  - ★ Cut 3 dark squares for 12 triangles
- ✪ C – Cut 2 dark squares 4 3/8". Cut each once on the diagonal to make 2 triangles.
- ✪ D – Cut one medium 5 3/8" square
- ✪ Sew all rotary cut pieces using a scant quarter-inch seam.

TO MAKE THE BLOCK

- ✪ Sew the four C pieces to the D square to make the center unit.

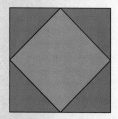

- ✪ Sew the B triangles together as shown.

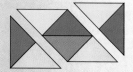

- ✪ Sew a triangle unit to either side of the center square.

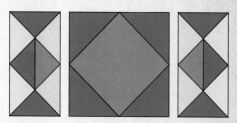

- ✪ Make the top and bottom row of the block by sewing an A square to either side of a triangle unit.

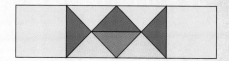

- ✪ Sew the strips together to complete the block.

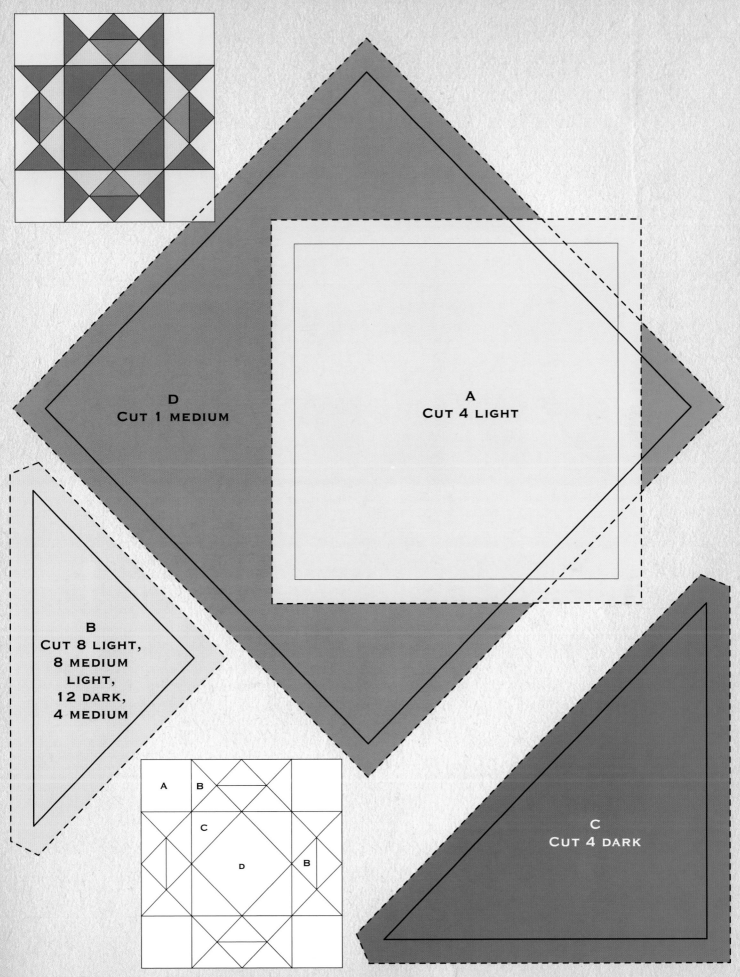

D
CUT 1 MEDIUM

A
CUT 4 LIGHT

B
CUT 8 LIGHT,
8 MEDIUM
LIGHT,
12 DARK,
4 MEDIUM

C
CUT 4 DARK

BLOCK 5
KANSAS TROUBLES

FOR MAHALA CHILDRESS DOYLE A SOUTHERN WIDOW

14" Finished Block

THE KANSAS TROUBLES BLOCK WAS MADE BY JEANNE POORE, OVERLAND PARK, KANSAS.

IN 1855, MAHALA Doyle came with her husband and six children to the Kansas Territory from Tennessee, a slave state. Mahala later recalled they were looking for a new start in a "free state where there would be no slave labor to hinder white men from making a fair day's wages." They found land near Pottawatomie Creek in eastern Kansas with Northern neighbors who never trusted them. Cultural and political differences quickly made enemies of Kansans from different backgrounds.

In 1856, a group of proslavery raiders attacked Lawrence, center of the territory's antislavery movement. New Yorker John Brown and his sons, determined to obtain revenge on Southerners—any Southerners—attacked the Doyle's cabin in the middle of the night. They dragged James Doyle and three of his sons out into the yard. Mahala begged them to spare John who was seventeen. They granted that one wish but hacked the other Doyle men to death.

Official blame for the Pottawatomie Massacre wasn't levied for decades but the Doyle family knew which of their neighbors were in the gang. Three years later Mahala, living in Chattanooga, heard of John Brown again when he led a murderous raid on a federal arsenal in Harper's Ferry, Virginia, hoping to incite a slave rebellion.

Above: Kansas Troubles by Karla Menaugh, machine quilted by Cherie Ralston, Lawrence, Kansas, 1998. To get the same effect, piece 16 blocks and add a 9" border for a 75" square quilt. Use many large-scale prints as well as smaller calicoes for an old-fashioned chintz quilt look.

John Brown. Some view him as a hero; others as a terrorist. Questions about Brown's place in history depend on one's views about the means to the end. Mahala Doyle's descendents still look back on her experience in Kansas with horror. Illustration courtesy of the Library of Congress.

John Brown

While Brown was in jail awaiting a sentence of execution, she sent him a powerful and bitter letter, telling him of her continuing rage and grief over the loss of her husband and children.

Brown's defenders always denied he'd killed the Doyles or anyone else. They branded the letter a forgery, accusing Mahala of being too ignorant to write such an eloquent indictment. Mahala remained in Chattanooga. The 1860 census finds her working as a maid to support her surviving children.

"Hotel de Dutton!" In 1867, Alexander Gardner photographed this inn near the Missouri and Kansas border and its guests. The woman in a sunbonnet seems to be keeping her eye on her stove, a heavy piece of baggage. A dozen years after the Doyle family's arrival, buildings in rural Kansas remained quite primitive.

She occasionally received money from some of Brown's supporters. A quilting friend is one of her descendants and she remembers her mother's story that as a small child she was introduced to an old and bearded "Uncle Johnny," a frightening apparition who became confused in her mind with his attacker John Brown. The little girl shrieked in terror. In that family, as in many other American families, sad stories of the Civil War are still passed on.

Kansas Troubles is an old pattern, dating back to the days of the Border Wars between Missouri and Kansas. This name was first recorded about 1890 by the Ladies Art Company, a pattern source from St. Louis. Whether women of Mahala Doyle's generation knew the pattern as Kansas Troubles is unknown.

Mahala Doyle's letter is now in the collection of the Gilder Lehrman Institute of American History.

CHATTANOOGA TENNESSEE
20TH NOVEMBER 1859

JOHN BROWN
SIR
ALTHO VENGEANCE IS NOT MINE, I CONFESS, THAT I DO FEEL GRATIFIED TO HEAR THAT YOU WARE STOPT IN YOUR FIENDISH CAREER AT HARPER'S FERRY, WITH THE LOSS OF YOUR TWO SONS, YOU CAN NOW APPRECIATE MY DISTRESS, IN KANSAS, WHEN YOU THEN AND THERE ENTERED MY HOUSE AT MIDNIGHT AND ARRESTED MY HUSBAND AND TWO BOYS AND TOOK THEM OUT OF THE YARD AND IN COLD

An artist for Frank Leslie's Newspaper depicted Brown on a sickbed at his trial for the attack at Harper's Ferry in 1859. He was hung a few weeks later.

BLOOD SHOT THEM DEAD IN MY HEARING, YOU CANT SAY YOU DONE IT TO FREE OUR SLAVES, WE HAD NONE AND NEVER EXPECTED TO OWN ONE, BUT HAS ONLY MADE ME A POOR DISCONSOLATE WIDOW WITH HELPLESS CHILDREN WHILE I FEEL FOR YOUR FOLLY. I DO HOPE & TRUST THAT YOU WILL MEET YOUR JUST REWARD. O HOW IT PAINED MY HEART TO HEAR THE DYING GROANS OF MY HUSBAND AND CHILDREN IF THIS SCRAWL GIVE YOU ANY CONSOLATION YOU ARE WELCOME TO IT.

MAHALA DOYLE

NB MY SON JOHN DOYLE WHOSE LIFE I BEGGED OF [YOU] IS NOW GROWN UP AND IS VERY DESIROUS TO BE AT CHARLESTON ON THE DAY OF YOUR EXECUTION WOULD CERTAINLY BE THERE IF HIS MEANS WOULD PERMIT IT THAT HE MIGHT ADJUST THE ROPE AROUND YOUR NECK IF GOV[ERNOR] WISE WOULD PERMIT IT.

ROTARY CUTTING

✪ A – Cut squares 2 5/8". Cut each in half to make 2 triangles.
  ★ Cut 12 dark squares to make 24 triangles.
  ★ Cut 8 light squares to make 16 triangles.

✪ B – Cut medium squares 4 3/8". Cut each in half to make 2 triangles.
  ★ Cut 2 medium squares to make 4 triangles.

✪ C – Cut light squares 7 7/8". Cut each in half to make 2 triangles.
  ★ Cut 2 light squares to make 4 triangles.

✪ D – Cut 4 light squares 2 1/4".

TO MAKE THE BLOCK

✪ Sew a dark triangle to a light triangle to make half-square triangles (HST). Make 16. Sew the HST together in pairs. Four pair must be a mirror image of the others as shown.

✪ Sew 1 pair to one side of piece B. Add a dark triangle to the unit as shown.

✪ Sew a dark A triangle to one end of a pair of HST, then sew a light D square to the other end. Sew this strip to the side of the B triangle.

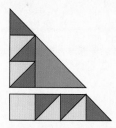

✪ Add triangle C next. Make four of these units and stitch them together to complete the block as shown on the next page.

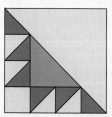

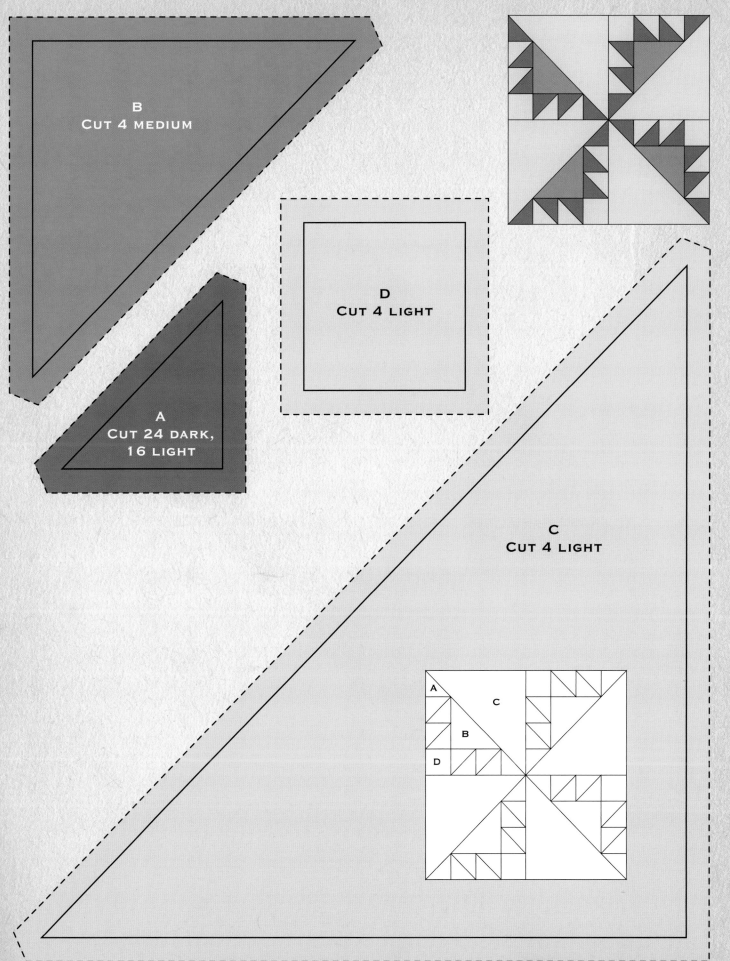

B
CUT 4 MEDIUM

A
CUT 24 DARK,
16 LIGHT

D
CUT 4 LIGHT

C
CUT 4 LIGHT

A

C

B

D

BLOCK 6

UNDERGROUND RAILROAD

FOR CLARINA I.H. NICHOLS
AN ABOLITIONIST

14" Finished Block

THE UNDERGROUND RAILROAD BLOCK WAS MADE BY PAT MOORE, KANSAS CITY, KANSAS.

WHEN NEW ENGLANDER Clarina Nichols, came to Kansas in 1855 with her husband, George, and their eleven-year-old son, the family had already gained fame for their antislavery newspaper published in Brattleboro, Vermont. As editor, Clarina was a scandal at a time when many women "scribbled" but few managed periodicals. She also lectured in favor of temperance, women's suffrage and the immediate abolishment of slavery, a position called abolitionism. Diarist Sara Robinson, who met her when she arrived in Kansas, described Clarina as an "editress and earnest worker for the rights of women."

When George Nichols died soon after their arrival, Clarina moved to the town of Quindaro within the boundaries of today's Kansas City, Kansas. The new settlement on the Missouri River was developed in a spot just west of the bend where the river takes its most easternmost "bite" out of Missouri, a place that offered runaway slaves a refuge south of Parkville. Clarina described Quindaro as one of the "most convenient stations on the Underground Rail Road." There she continued her fight for "emancipation without proclamation" as an editor at the newspaper, the *Chindowan*.

Above: Clarina I. H. Nichols

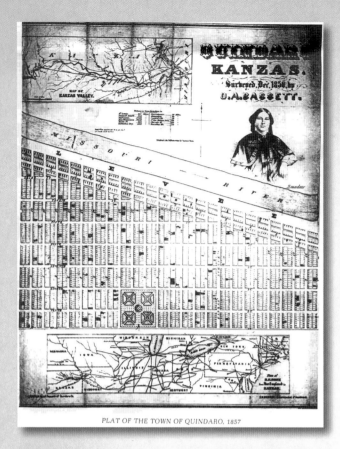

PLAT OF THE TOWN OF QUINDARO, 1857

Clarina guided Caroline down into her cistern, furnished with "comforters, pillow and chair." A washtub and laundry tools were placed over the trapdoor to disguise it but Caroline couldn't stay quiet. "Poor Caroline, trembling and almost paralyzed with fear of discovery, her nerves weakened by grieving for her little girl transported to Texas, and the cruel blows which had broken her arm and scarred her body—could not be left alone through the night." Clarina hid in the cistern with her until morning when the posse of slave hunters left town. "When evening fell again Caroline...found a safe conveyance to Leavenworth friends."

Underground Railroad is a quilt pattern with many other names, among them Jacob's Ladder and Stepping Stones. The earliest quilts in the design go back to the 1890s when Clarina Nichols and others were writing their memoirs of the Civil War and the Underground Railroad.

This map of Quindaro shows an ambitious plan for a city that lost its reason to exist with the end of slavery. The portrait is of Nancy Quindaro Brown Guthrie, the Wyandot woman who negotiated with her relatives for the land under the town. Quindaro became part of Kansas City, Kansas, and disappeared over the years as its buildings fell prey to the Missouri's regular floods.

TO READ MORE ABOUT CLARINA NICHOLS:

Diane Eickhoff, *Revolutionary Heart: The Life of Clarina Nichols and the Pioneering Crusade for Women's Rights* (Kansas City, Kansas: Quindaro Press, 2006)

She later recalled an escape in Quindaro. "One beautiful evening late in October, '61, as twilight was fading from the bluff, a hurried message came to me from our neighbor....'You must hide Caroline. Fourteen slave hunters are camped on the Park.'"

Path to Freedom *by Karla Menaugh and Barbara Brackman, Lawrence, Kansas, 2000. 54" square.*
Karla and I took four patches and triangles from the Underground Railroad block and added a Sawtooth Star to represent the North Star. We hand quilted it using the old-fashioned "big stitch" and crochet cotton.

ROTARY CUTTING

- ✪ A – Cut squares 2 7/8"
  - ★ Cut 10 light and 10 medium
- ✪ B – Cut squares 5 1/2" and cut each once on the diagonal to make 2 triangles.
  - ★ Cut 2 light squares to make 4 triangles.
  - ★ Cut 2 dark squares to make 4 triangles.

TO MAKE THE BLOCK

- ✪ Make five 4-patch units by sewing the light A squares to the medium B squares as shown.

- ✪ Sew the light B triangles to the dark B triangles.

- ✪ Sew a 4-patch unit to a half-square triangle unit. Then add another 4-patch to complete the first row. Make two strips like this, one for the top row, the other for the bottom row.

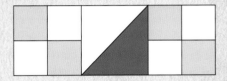

- ✪ For the center row, sew a half-square triangle unit to either side of a 4-patch unit.

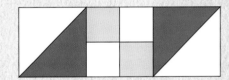

- ✪ Sew the three rows together to complete the block.

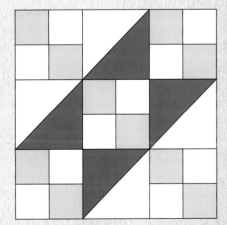

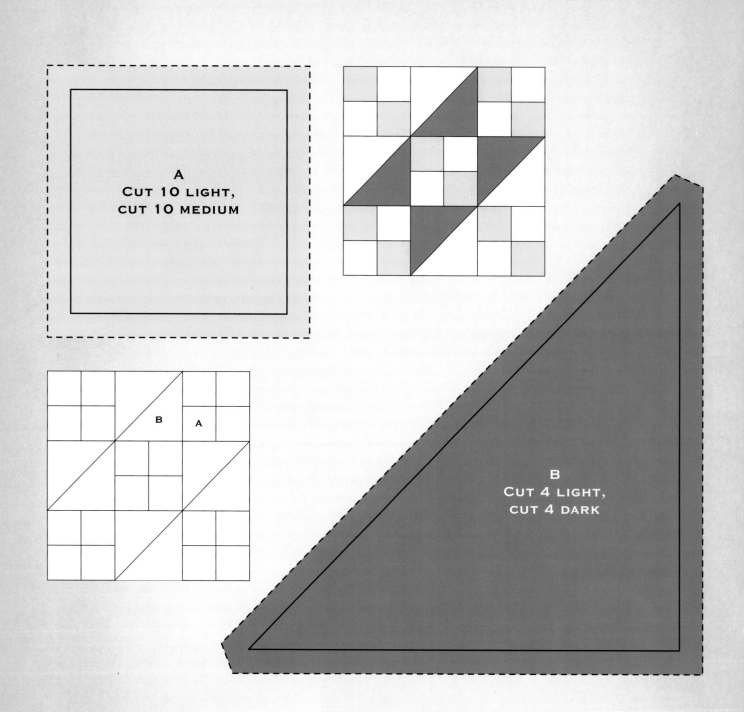

A
Cut 10 light,
cut 10 medium

B

A

B
Cut 4 light,
cut 4 dark

PROJECT 2
MYSTERY TRAIN

21" x 29 1/2" · 6" Block · 3" Border

MYSTERY TRAIN, BY BARBARA BRACKMAN, LAWRENCE, KANSAS, 2007.
I THOUGHT MYSTERY TRAIN, AN OLD RHYTHM AND BLUES SONG FROM SUN RECORDS, MIGHT
BE A GOOD NAME FOR THIS MYSTERIOUS VARIATION OF THE UNDERGROUND RAILROAD
BLOCK, ADAPTED FROM THE BLUE AND WHITE ANTIQUE. IT'S PIECED USING TWO DIFFERENT
BLOCKS, ONE AN UNDERGROUND RAILROAD OR JACOB'S LADDER BLOCK, THE OTHER A
SQUARE WITH TWO OF THE CORNERS REPLACED WITH TRIANGLES.

YOU NEED

- ✪ 6 blocks in the Underground Railroad design
- ✪ 2 alternate blocks
- ✪ 4 pieced side setting triangles
- ✪ 4 triangles for the corners
- ✪ 2 setting triangles for the top and bottom
- ✪ Fabric
    - ★ 1/4 yard light for Underground Railroad blocks
    - ★ 1/2 yard dark scraps
    - ★ 1/2 yard contrasting fabric for alternate and setting triangles
    - ★ 3/8 yard for border
    - ★ 4 strips for straight binding or 1 fat quarter for continuous bias

ROTARY CUTTING

- ✪ A – Cut squares 2 7/8". Cut each in half diagonally to make 2 triangles. For each Underground Railroad block cut 2 light and 2 dark squares to make 4 light and 4 dark triangles.
    - ★ For each of the two alternate blocks cut 1 dark square to make 2 triangles.
    - ★ For the pieced side triangles cut 2 dark squares to make 4 triangles.

- ✪ B – Cut squares 1 1/2". For each Underground Railroad block, cut 10 dark squares and 10 light squares.

- ✪ C – Cut a medium 6 1/2" square. Cut the corners off using the template. You need 2 squares for the alternate blocks that run down the center.

- ✪ D – For the pieced side triangles, use the template to cut 4 medium pieces
    - ★ For the small setting triangles in the corners of the quilt, cut 2 medium 5 1/8" squares. Cut each once on the diagonal to make 2 triangles. You need 4 triangles.
    - ★ For the large setting triangles at the top and bottom center, cut 1 contrasting 9 3/4" square. Cut the square twice on the diagonal to make 4 triangles. You will have 2 triangles left over.

BORDERS

- ✪ Cut 2 strips 2 1/2" by 26" for the side borders
- ✪ Cut 2 strips 2 1/2" by 21 1/2" for the top and bottom borders

PIECING THE UNDERGROUND RAILROAD BLOCKS

- ✪ See the instructions on page 49 and piece 6 blocks following the coloring pattern in the illustration.

PIECING THE ALTERNATE BLOCKS AND PIECED SETTING TRIANGLES.

- ✪ Sew an A triangle to either side of piece C to make the 2 alternate blocks

- ✪ Sew an A triangle to the narrower side of piece D to create the 4 setting triangles.

SETTING THE QUILT

- ✪ Alternate the Underground Railroad blocks to the alternate blocks as shown by creating diagonal strips ending in large setting triangles.
- ✪ Add the corner triangles.
- ✪ Add the side borders, then the top and bottom borders.

QUILTING

Barbara hand quilted this piece in period fashion by quilting pairs of chevron shaped lines in the larger triangles. She outlined many areas and used the star on page 115 in the two large shapes in the center.

*Antique quilt in an unusual variation of the
Jacob's Ladder or Underground Railroad pattern.
Unknown maker, estimated date: 1890-1925. It
took a while to figure out the pattern here. It's
actually two blocks placed on point that look like a
strip quilt. I've seen one other like it, made about
the same time. In that one the blocks were placed on
the square forming shaded strips diagonally across
the quilt.*

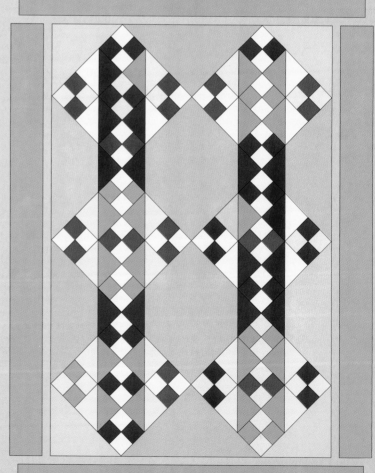

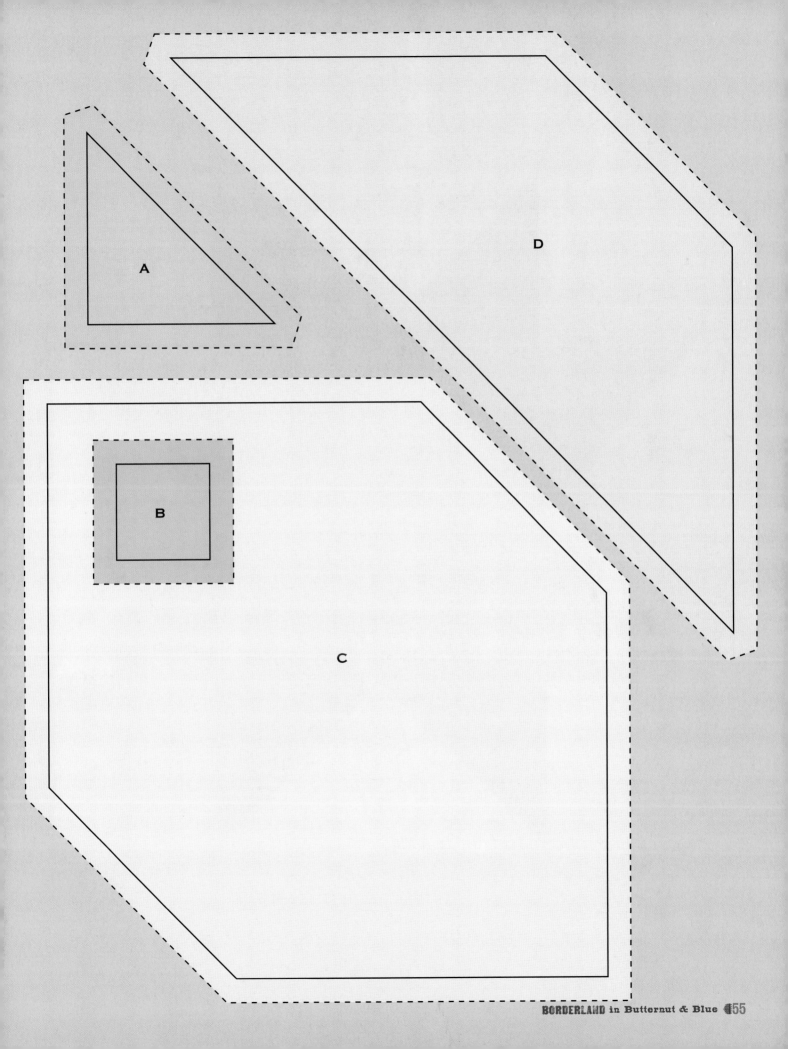

A

B

C

D

BLOCK 7
MISSOURI STAR
FOR MATTIE LYKINS BINGHAM
A SOUTHERN REBEL

14" Finished Block

THE MISSOURI STAR BLOCK IS MADE BY JEANNE POORE, OVERLAND PARK, KANSAS.

MISSOURI STAR RECALLS Mattie Lykins Bingham (1824-1890), Kansas City's own Secessionist spokeswoman. Born Martha A. Livingston in Kentucky, she was orphaned at three and reared by her grandmother and older sisters. As a poor young woman of good family, Mattie had few financial choices. In her teens, she pursued an acceptable option and taught school.

But Mattie was an unusual Southern belle, a published writer from an early age. We can trace her travels through her scrapbook of newspaper clippings, a copy of which is at the Kansas City Public Library. She accompanied

Above: Mattie Lykins Bingham.

her sister's family to Jefferson City where "The Forest Cottage," her serial story appeared in the local newspaper when she was 17 years old. The sisters moved to Lexington, Missouri, where "The Presentiment" was published in *The Weekly Express*. While she taught school there, Mattie sent letters to a Shelbyville, Kentucky, paper using a form popular at the time. Her humorous observations about life in the far west came from the perspective of a country bumpkin named Debby Doolittle lately of "Hard Scratch, Kanetuck."

She also spent time with a sister in Shelbyville

George Caleb Bingham's house in Arrow Rock before its first reconstruction in 1934. Photograph courtesy of the Library of Congress.

where she met Dr. Johnston Lykins, a missionary to the Shawnee in the Indian Territory. Lykins, a widower twenty-five years older than Mattie, wooed and won her. They spent a honeymoon year in Washington City and moved to the small town of Kansas, on the south side of the Missouri River.

As missionaries to the tribes, Lykins' family had been able to acquire prime real estate in Indian Territory and along the Missouri border. Few believed Lykins' rocky land at the foot of the bluffs on what is now Broadway would ever be worth much. The town of Kansas, situated between Independence on the river and the inland city of Westport, seemed destined to remain a minor outpost.

At the crest of the bluff, the Lykins built a small house surrounded by tall weeds and hazel brush. In her memoirs, Mattie remembered that Native Americans camped in the thickets were daily visitors.

Mattie took her place as one of society's leaders. She helped establish social order by organizing a sewing society and planning a traditional Christmas bazaar to sell handmade goods to earn money to warm, heat and carpet a new church. As mid-December cold descended, Mattie realized there wasn't a heated building large enough to contain the Ladies Fair, so with typical creativity she commandeered a steamboat stranded in the ice at the wharf and held a successful Christmas Eve fair that raised $500. "I venture to say that no fair held since in our city, in proportion to population, has ever excelled in its receipts the first fair held in Kansas City."

In later years she was often asked about the town's early history. "How did you manage to spend your time in those days? Your society must have been very much mixed and at a fearfully low ebb both morally and intellectually." She always answered that although "the circle of the best society" was small, the women kept their houses neat and clean, their children well dressed and well behaved, moral standards were kept high with no women of "unsavory reputation...ever permitted to enter that "charmed circle".

As the town of Kansas grew into the City of Kansas, Johnston Lykins prospered. He sold his lots and bought more, acted as Postmaster and Mayor and practiced medicine when he had the time. The 1860 census described him as a Bank President worth $60,000.

Although Mattie never had children of her own, the house was full of stepchildren, nephews, foster children and their friends. Laura Coates Reed who visited as a child recalled it as a typical Southern home, "concealed in a grove of stately forest trees...with spacious halls and apartments, presided over by a host and hostess of the old régime of Southern hospitality."

During the Civil War Mattie became known as a woman of opinions—most of them Secessionist. In January 1863, an Ohio newspaper published a letter from her that began "May God Bless you and save you unharmed from Black Republican rule...I grant it is not woman's province to array her name in a public journal on political questions." Woman's province was never a place that concerned her so she went on to detail the indignities of living under Lincoln's federal government.

A weathered angel stands guard over children on the hill that was once the site of the Lykins Institute, Mattie's orphanage.

Martha Lykins Bingham's grave stone lies on the ground between the monuments of her two husbands at Union Cemetery just out of sight behind Bingham's marker.

She saved her final salvo for the greatest indignity of all, the sight of black men in Union uniforms demanding respect from their former masters. "The women of Missouri stand aghast and feel we are at the mercy of those who are worse than savages. Negro boys from 12 years old and upwards are armed and dressed in the uniform of the U.S. soldiers, and with a swaggering, defiant air stalk our streets and if perchance they meet a lady she is forced to step aside and let the sable defenders of our Union and our Constitution have undisputed possession of the sidewalks."

Mattie was visiting her stepson in Lawrence the morning of Quantrill's Raid and many suspected her of helping the guerrillas, complicity she always denied. Her Southern sympathies made her a prime target for banishment under Order Number Eleven, which sent Southern partisans to Missouri's interior. Her Unionist husband remained in Kansas City.

After the War, Mattie returned to Kansas City and devoted the rest of her life to the Lost Cause,

beginning by raising money to "take up and bury the Confederate dead, who sleep beneath the sod in many desolate and waste places in Jackson County."

Her passions continued to cause controversy. One newspaper editor wrote, she "ought to be largely reorganized [and] fully reconstructed [and] let the Confederate dead, who have been properly killed and decently interred, alone." Her advocacy for honorable burials resulted in a Confederate Cemetery near what is now the corner of Gregory Boulevard and Troost.

She then turned her efforts to an orphanage for children of the Confederate dead. In 1874, Mattie and other Southern sympathizers including Sarah Davis Johnson and Eliza Thomas Bingham lobbied the Missouri Legislature into funding a "Home for Destitute Widows and Orphans" on about 40 acres near 32nd and Locust, another charity that pitted Butternuts against Union Blues. The public debate prompted the Legislature to reverse its decision and withdraw support after only a year. By 1881, the home was bankrupt, and was sold at a foreclosure auction to the Little Sisters of the Poor. Johnston Lykins had filed for bankruptcy in 1874 a month after the cornerstone for the Orphan's Home was laid. He died two years later.

The same year that Mattie was widowed Eliza Bingham, her colleague in Confederate charities, also died. In 1878, Mattie married Eliza's husband George Caleb Bingham, a well-known artist and one-time Union officer, who served during the War as Missouri's civilian treasurer. Although a Union official, Bingham sympathized with Missouri's pro-Southern citizens. His paintings titled "Martial Law" or "Order Number 11" depicting their anguish are lasting images of the Border Wars.

Bingham died soon after their marriage and Mattie spent the 1880s caring for young relatives and foster children from the orphanage. She died in her mid-sixties after cancer surgery, leaving a will crafted to continue her work after her death. She dictated that her only assets, George Caleb Bingham's paintings and prints, be auctioned to fund the Confederate Home in Higginsville, Missouri.

Mattie is buried in the Union Cemetery next to her last husband and near her first, far from the Confederate Cemetery she helped to found.

Missouri Star, published in the *Chicago Tribune* in the 1930s, reminds us of the formidable Mattie Lykins Bingham, a woman Laura Coates Reed remembered as "whole-souled and big-hearted."

VISIT

Bingham-Waggoner estate. George Caleb Bingham and his second wife Eliza lived here in Independence between 1864 and 1870. The house, located at 313 W. Pacific Avenue, was remodeled by the Waggoner family into a late Victorian showcase.

The Bingham House at Arrow Rock was reconstructed as an 1830s Federal-style home echoing the building's appearance when Bingham built it in 1836.

Union Cemetery, where many of Kansas City's Union veterans and Mattie Lykins Bingham are buried.

See the Confederate Cemetery that Mattie worked so hard to develop. It's now known as Forest Hill Calvary Cemetery. Look for the Confederate Monument on the southern side near East Gregory Boulevard.

Visit another of Mattie's charities, the Confederate Home in Higginsville, Missouri. The cemetery and buildings are now the Confederate Memorial State Historic Site, a Missouri state park.

ROTARY CUTTING FOR MISSOURI STAR

- ✪ A – Cut 4 light 4" squares
- ✪ B – Cut 2 dark 4 3/8" squares. Cut each square on the diagonal to make 2 triangles.
- ✪ C – Cut 1 light 8 1/4" square and cut into 4 triangles by cutting twice on the diagonal.
- ✪ D – Cut squares 4 3/4". Cut each into 4 triangles by cutting twice on the diagonal.
  - ★ Cut 2 dark squares to make 8 triangles.
  - ★ Cut 2 medium squares to make 8 triangles.
- ✪ E – Cut 1 medium 5 1/2" square.

TO MAKE THE BLOCK

- ✪ Sew the medium blue D triangles to the dark blue D triangles.

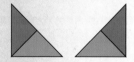

- ✪ Sew the D triangle units to each side of the light C triangles. Make 4 units like this. We'll call these the DC units for clarity.

- ✪ Sew the dark blue B triangles to the sides of the E square as shown.

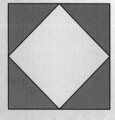

- ✪ Make three rows for the block. The first and last rows are made by sewing an A square to one side of the DC unit, then adding another A square to the other side.

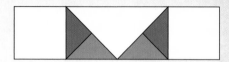

- ✪ The center row is made by sewing a DC unit to either side of the center square.

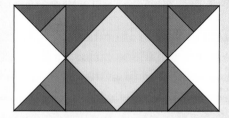

- ✪ Sew the rows together to complete the block.

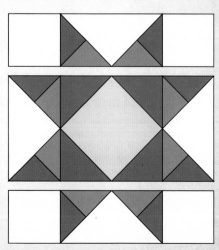

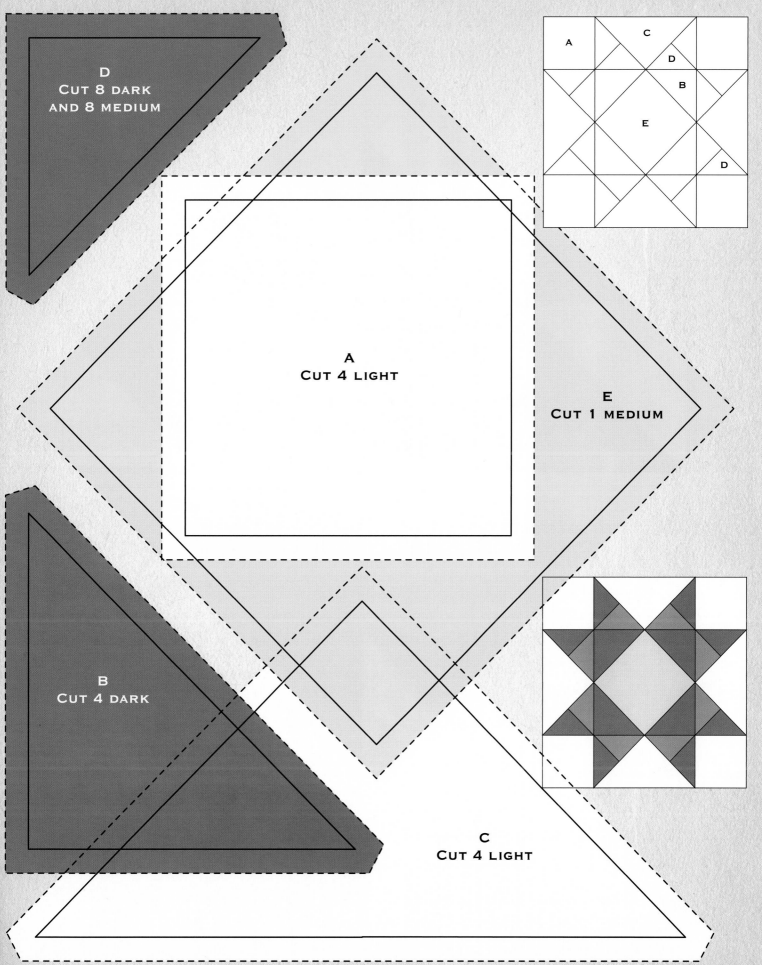

D
CUT 8 DARK
AND 8 MEDIUM

A
CUT 4 LIGHT

E
CUT 1 MEDIUM

B
CUT 4 DARK

C
CUT 4 LIGHT

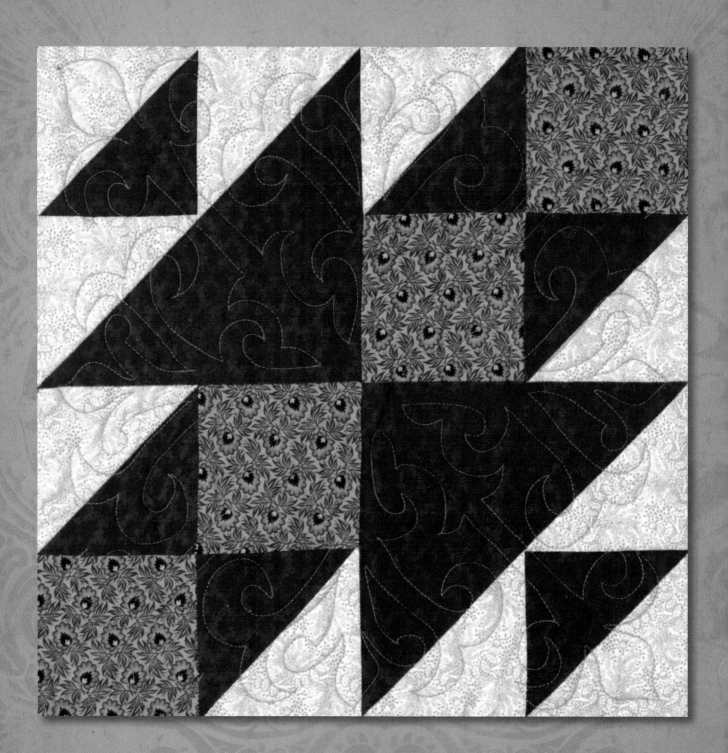

BLOCK 8

CROSSES AND LOSSES

FOR CHARITY MCCORKLE KERR
A MARTYR

14" Finished Block

THE CROSSES AND LOSSES BLOCK WAS MADE BY JEANNE POORE, OVERLAND PARK, KANSAS.

ONCE THE CIVIL War began, hostility between proslavery Missourians and free-state Kansans hardened along Confederate and Union lines. Federal troops and urban politicians held Missouri for the Union despite strong Confederate sentiments among people along the western border. Missouri's countryside bled from an intensive guerrilla war fought between the irregular Confederate sympathizers known as Bushwhackers and the Jayhawkers some of whom were genuinely pro-union and some who simply pretended to be.

The bushwhackers were primarily young men, some acting out of patriotism, others for revenge and a few for the thrill of violence. They lived in caves along creeks and rivers like the Sni-A-Bar and the Little Blue. Women—their sisters, mothers and sweethearts—aided them by supplying food, medical care and hand-embroidered garments known as guerrilla shirts.

During the violent summer of 1863, in an effort to starve the Bushwhackers out of hiding, Union soldiers arrested women suspected of harboring them, among them Charity McCorkle Kerr (1831-

Above: Sisters-in-law Charity McCorkle Kerr and Nannie Harris, about 1860. Courtesy of the State Historical Society of Missouri.

A tangle of scrub on the Blue River's banks looks much as it did when butternut guerrillas camped.

1863) and her sister-in-law Nannie McCorkle. Their crime was trading a load of grain for barrels of flour in Kansas City.

Charity's brother John McCorkle was a guerrilla fighter, as was her husband Nathan Kerr. Nannie was the widow of another brother Jabez McCorkle who'd died in a few months earlier after accidentally shooting himself. With no medical care, he lingered in the woods for two weeks before dying of infection.

The women were held in a makeshift jail in a stone building on Grand Avenue between Fourteenth and Fifteenth Streets. George Caleb Bingham had recently inherited the building from his father-in-law's estate and added a third story studio. The Union Army commandeered his studio to hold a group of female prisoners—

accounts vary from seven to seventeen, an indication of the vagueness of the historical accounts.

After showing signs of instability for several days, the building and the one next to it collapsed on August 13, 1863, killing Charity and at least two others, Josephine Anderson and Armenia Whitsett Gilvey. Several others were injured— again the number and names are unclear. Many Missouri families devastated by the disaster had sons in the bushwhacker armies. Brothers, husbands and cousins were enraged at what many still see as a conspiracy to execute the women. Some say the jail collapse was the fuse that fired the vengeful raid in Lawrence a week later when William Quantrill and hundreds of Missourians burned the city to the ground.

Falling of a Female Prison.
FOUR WOMEN KILLED—SIX WOUNDED.

KANSAS CITY, Saturday, Aug. 15.
The Female Prison in this place fell in on
Thursday morning, burying in the ruins eleven
women. Four were killed, one mortally wounded,
and six slightly injured.

The site of the makeshift jail near the corner of Grand Boulevard and Truman Road is no longer visible. It's under the new Sprint Center that covers eight and a half acres between Grand and Oak Street in Kansas City.

Crosses and Losses, reminding us of the deaths of Charity Kerr and the other young women, is a traditional block given that name in Ruth Finley's 1929 book, *Old Patchwork Quilts*.

Josephine Anderson's memorial at the Union Cemetery. Josephine's brother was known as Bloody Bill Anderson, one of the most vicious of the bushwhackers.

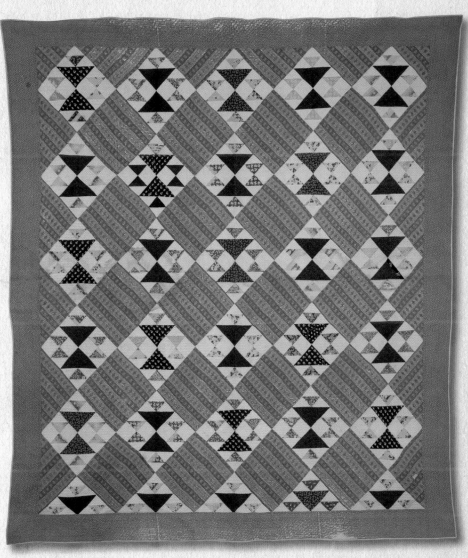

This Crosses and Losses antique quilt was purchased in Missouri. Its estimated date is 1840-1860. The old pattern was also published in the early twentieth century under the names Double X and Fox and Geese.

ROTARY CUTTING FOR CROSSES AND LOSSES

- ✪ A – Cut 4 medium 4" squares.
- ✪ B – Cut squares 4 3/8". Cut each once on the diagonal to make 2 triangles.
  - ★ Cut 3 dark squares to make 6 triangles
  - ★ Cut 5 light squares to make 10 triangles.
- ✪ C – Cut 1 dark 7 7/8" square. Cut once on the diagonal to make 2 triangles.

TO MAKE THE BLOCK

- ✪ Sew a light B triangle to a dark B triangle thus making a half-square triangle.

- ✪ Add a light B triangle to two sides of the half-square triangle.

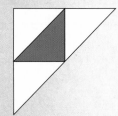

- ✪ Sew a dark blue C triangle to the pieces you just put together. You will be sewing on the diagonal. This makes up the upper left corner of the block as well as the lower right so you need to make two of these units.

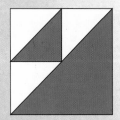

- ✪ Sew the remaining light and dark B triangles together to make half-square triangles.

- ✪ Sew a half-square triangle unit to a medium A square. Now sew a medium A square to a half-square triangle unit. Sew the two rows together to make the upper right quarter. Make another unit like this for the lower left quarter.

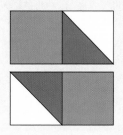

- ✪ Sew the four quarters together to complete the block.

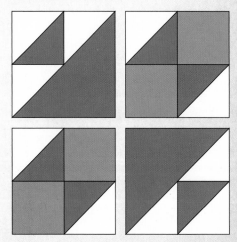

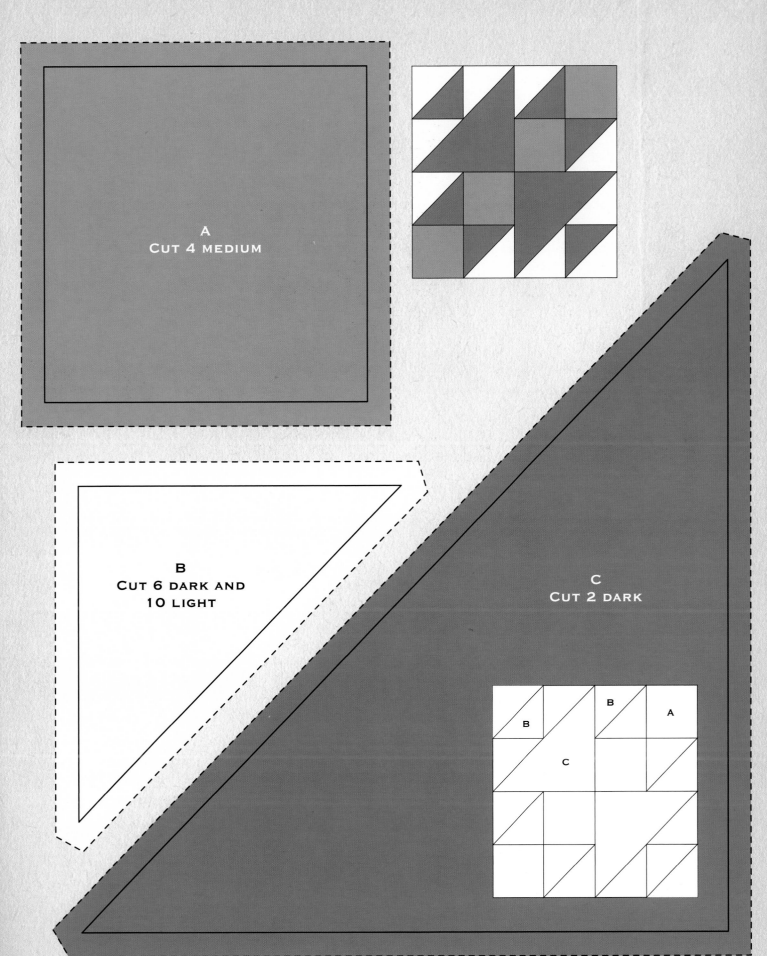

A
Cut 4 medium

B
Cut 6 dark and
10 light

C
Cut 2 dark

B

B

A

C

BLOCK 9

MOTHER'S DREAM

FOR ELIZABETH MCMAHON SPEER
A GRIEVING MOTHER

14" Finished Block
THE MOTHER'S DREAM BLOCK WAS MADE BY PAT MOORE, KANSAS CITY, KANSAS.

IN 1855, ELIZABETH McMahon Speer (1822 - 1876) came to Kansas with five children under the age of ten and her husband, John, an antislavery newspaper man. She was considered outspoken in her own right. When her husband's Lawrence newspaper outraged the proslavery Kansas government, a group of federal troops and Missouri civilians came to arrest John. Sara Robinson described the scene:

"The house of Mr. Speer had been repeatedly searched for him. [The Sheriff] approached the house waving a hammer to show his valor... he was greeted by a dish of hot water in his face. Mrs. Speer then said, 'I have respect for the U.S. troops... but as for this puke of a Missourian he shall not come in.' The troops enjoyed this unceremonious salutation given by the Ohio lady to the brave official."

"Pukes" was a none-too-delicate nickname for Missourians. The story of Elizabeth Speer insulting the Sheriff was retold as early Lawrence folklore. As the years went by, the epithet "Puke" was exchanged for the slightly more decorous "Border Ruffian".

The Missourians got their revenge seven years later on the morning of August 21st, 1863. Elizabeth, pregnant with her last child,

Above: The Speer family, probably in the early 1870s, Elizabeth is wearing black in the center. Husband John stands in the back row slightly to the right. Photograph courtesy of the Hobbs Park Memorial.

News of the Lawrence massacre was telegraphed to newspapers around the nation. This engraving from Harper's Weekly is dramatic but the only exaggeration seems to be the height of the buildings behind the smoke.

was awakened by gunshots and hooting from hundreds of bushwhackers under the leadership of William Quantrill. Before the morning was over, two of her sons had been murdered. Her second son's body was never found.

She set a place for the missing boy every night for the remaining 13 years of her life. John put her grief into words in an advertisement he printed daily for months after Quantrill's Raid, asking for any information about Robert:

"The people well know that my son was killed in the Lawrence Massacre...It was a terrible stroke to his parents to part with that dear boy. But a sadder affliction was the loss of our second son Robert Speer, whose body has never been found....As [he was] known to be very anxious to join the army, some think [he] may have pursued Quantrill. His mother...dreams of him in a handsome blue soldier's dress and hopes ever against hope that he may live."

A different portrait of Elizabeth's grief emerged in a 1933 *Kansas City Star* interview with A.P. Elder, who was about 10 years old and living in Ottawa during the Lawrence raid. He remembered the trial of William Maddox, the only Missourian prosecuted for the attack. The venue was moved to Ottawa due to the natural prejudice of the citizens of Lawrence and Elizabeth Speer stayed in his home so she could observe the trial.

"I heard her tell how her two sons were murdered and I saw the bitter tears she shed and noted the grim compression of her lips when she declared at our table that Maddox should not escape, and I saw her take her two revolvers each morning as she went to the trial. Maddox had a dozen witnesses from Olathe who swore that he started with Quantrill in the raid on Lawrence, but was taken desperately sick on the way and stopped off in Olathe. ..There was no question that this was the truth, but Mrs. Speer declared that he should not escape anyway....if it was acquittal she would be the executioner anyhow."

Almost 200 men and boys were killed in Quantrill's Raid on Lawrence

Elizabeth's terrible revenge was frustrated when the verdict clearing Maddox was read while she slept.

"Mrs. Maddox... as determined a woman as Mrs. Speer... had secretly brought two fast horses from Missouri and had them tethered in the alley back of the courthouse. The moment the verdict came in, Maddox slipped out....I shall never forget the rage of Mrs. Speer when she was awakened and told what happened. She finally slumped down in an arm chair and gave herself to sobs that her two boys, murdered as they had been, and their bodies burned, should go unavenged."

Mother's Dream was published by Kansas City's Aunt Martha pattern company in the 1930s. Add some dark blue to the block to remember Elizabeth Speer's dream that her missing boy was somewhere safe, wearing a Union uniform.

VISIT

The Hobbs Park Memorial, a park devoted to the memory of John and Elizabeth Speer on the site of their former farm in Lawrence, Kansas, at 10th and Delaware.

The garden at the Hobbs Park Memorial in Lawrence, Kansas, is dedicated to Elizabeth Speer. This house has been moved to the Speer's farmstead.

ROTARY CUTTING

- ❂ A – Cut 5 medium 3 3/4" squares.
- ❂ B – Cut squares 3 1/8". Cut once on the diagonal to make 2 triangles.
  - ★ 8 light squares to make 16 triangles.
  - ★ 2 dark squares to make 4 triangles.
- ❂ C – Cut squares 2 3/8". Cut once on the diagonal to make 2 triangles.
  - ★ 12 light squares to make 24 triangles.
  - ★ 12 dark squares to make 24 triangles.
- ❂ D – Cut 4 medium 2" x 5 1/8" rectangles.

TO MAKE THE BLOCK

- ❂ Sew the B triangles to the A squares thus making square-in-a-square units. The center A square will be surrounded by dark triangles and the four corner squares will be surrounded by light triangles.

- ❂ Sew the light C triangles to the dark C triangles to make half-square triangle units. You will need a total of 24 half-square triangles.

- ❂ Sew three half-square triangles to either side of the dark D rectangles. The darkest part of the half-square triangles should always touch the rectangle. We'll call this the CD unit for clarity.

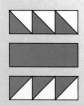

- ❂ Sew a square-in-a-square unit to either side of a CD unit. Make two rows like this.

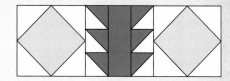

- ❂ Sew a CD unit to either side of the square-in-square unit that is surrounded by dark triangles. This is the center row.

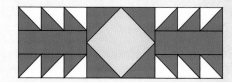

- ❂ Sew the rows together.

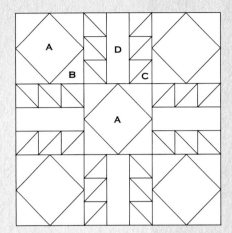

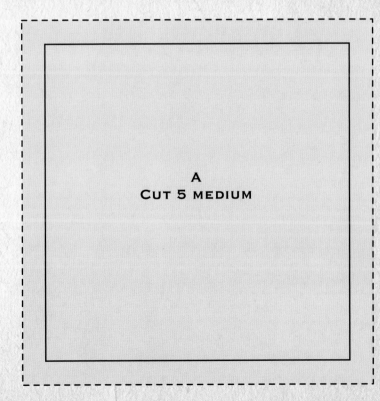

D
CUT 4 DARK

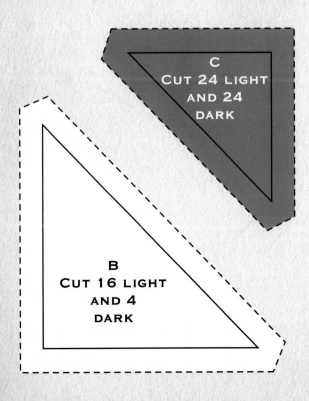

C
CUT 24 LIGHT AND 24 DARK

B
CUT 16 LIGHT AND 4 DARK

A
CUT 5 MEDIUM

PROJECT 3
DOGTOOTH SUNFLOWER

40" x 40" · 16" Blocks · 4" finished border

DOGTOOTH SUNFLOWER, DESIGNED BY BARBARA BRACKMAN, MACHINE APPLIQUÉD BY KARLA MENAUGH, LA GRANGE, KENTUCKY, QUILTED BY LORI KUKUK, MCLOUTH, KANSAS, 2006.

THE SUNFLOWER IS THE OFFICIAL KANSAS STATE FLOWER AND HAS BEEN FOR A HUNDRED YEARS OR SO. THE LEGISLATURE CHOSE IT BECAUSE IT'S A NATIVE PLANT THAT THRIVES ON THE PLAINS AND PROVIDES WELCOME COLOR IN THE DUSTY LATE SUMMER LANDSCAPE. WE THOUGHT A SUNFLOWER QUILT WOULD MAKE A GOOD MEMORIAL TO THE KANSAS PIONEER WOMEN---TRANSPLANTS WHO THRIVED HERE TOO.

THIS FOUR-BLOCK QUILT, based on antique sunflower designs, has a dogtooth border---spiky triangles that are appliquéd rather than pieced. Dogtooth appliqué is an old technique. Some of the earliest American patchwork quilts feature these triangular borders, made with a strip of fabric that is slashed and turned under. The sunflowers and stars could be made in similar fashion, cutting circles, slashing the edges and folding the points rather than using a template. We give you templates but see page 78 for instructions for the old-fashioned dogtooth appliqué technique.

YOU NEED
- ✪ 4 appliqued blocks
- ✪ 1 appliqued border finishing to 4"

FABRIC FOR THE APPLIQUE

Karla Menaugh always does a great job of combining plaids and prints, bright colors and muted shades to create her own version of the folk/primitive look. To obtain her scrappy palette, use scraps of yellow-gold, dark brown and medium green prints and woven plaids and stripes for the stars.

- ✪ For a more unified look buy a fat quarter each:
  - ★ yellow-gold
  - ★ dark brown
  - ★ medium green
  - ★ light blue plaid
  - ★ red plaid or stripe

FABRIC FOR THE BACKGROUND AND BORDER
- ✪ 2 yards of blue for the background
- ✪ 1 yard of butternut brown plaid for the border appliqué and binding
- ✪ Cut the borders first and then cut bias strips for the binding

CUTTING DIRECTIONS

FOR THE BLOCKS

- ✪ Cut 4 blue 16 1/2" squares for the background of the appliqué blocks.
- ✪ Using the templates, cut the appliqué pieces as indicated on the templates, adding seam allowances of a scant quarter inch.

FOR THE BORDERS

- ✪ For the background border, cut 4 blue strips 4 1/2" x 41".
- ✪ For the dogtooth border cut 4 plaid strips 2 1/2" x 41".

SEWING THE BLOCKS

- ✪ Fold and press the background square into triangular quarters so you will have a guide for appliqué placement.
- ✪ Prepare the appliqué pieces by turning the edges under and basting or gluing the seam allowances in place.
- ✪ Place the pieces as shown in the illustration and baste or glue them in place. Note the sunflower heads are a little bit off center to give them a natural look. Leave the center star off until you've set the blocks.

- ✪ Stitch the blocks using your favorite hand or machine method.

SETTING THE BLOCKS

- ✪ Sew pairs of blocks as shown with the stems pointing to the center of the quilt and the stars along the outside edge.

- ✪ Stitch these pairs to make a four-block quilt.
- ✪ Applique the center star over the seams in the very center

APPLIQUEING THE DOGTOOTH BORDER.

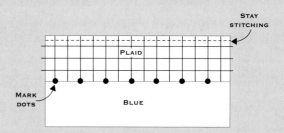

- ✪ Stay stitch the plaid strip to the edge of the blue background strip.

- ✪ Mark dots every 1 3/4" on the free edge of the plaid strip.
- ✪ Cut slits 1 1/2" long at each dot.

- ✪ Fold and applique each tooth.
- ✪ After the borders are appliqued, add them to the quilt with the plaid triangles along the outer edge.

- ✪ Miter the corners.

- ✪ The dogtooth triangles will probably meet in an irregular fashion at the miters (see Barbara's Dogtooth border on page 90 for an irregular look). If you prefer a regular corner like Karla's, cut corner triangles of plaid fabric and add them over the edge of the corners. To cut these corners cut 2 squares 5 1/8" of plaid and cut each into two triangles.

QUILTING

Lori Kukuk machine-quilted a scroll design in the blue background and added natural lines like veins in the leaves and a curvy kind of grid to represent the sunflower seeds.

OPTIONAL HAND-APPLIQUE METHOD

DOGTOOTH FLOWERS AND STARS

Many nineteenth century quilts with a terrific folksy look were made using this method. Flowers and stars—five, six or eight pointed stars---were easily cut from circles.

THE YELLOW PETALS IN THE SUNFLOWERS

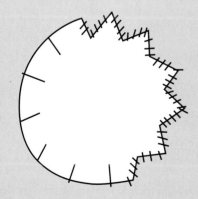

- ✪ Cut 4 yellow circles, each with a diameter of 7 1/2" using the template A-X (optional)
- ✪ Do not add a seam allowance.
- ✪ Prepare the yellow circles by snipping 12 cuts, each an inch long, around the edge as shown on the template.

- ✪ Begin by the block by hand appliquéing the sunflower petals. Fold under the sunflower petals ahead of yourself as you sew. Tuck in the threads in the V cut with your needle as you move through the flower. Put an extra stitch or two in the V cut and fold the next petal in.
- ✪ Remember to leave a spot for the stem.
- ✪ Once you've stitched this down, add the stems, leaves and brown center circle using conventional applique.

THE STARS.

- ✪ Cut 13 plaid and striped circles, each with a diameter of 3 1/4" using template E-X (optional).

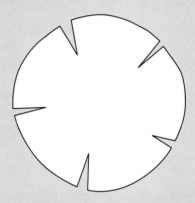

- ✪ Prepare the circle by snipping 5 cuts each 3/4" long around the edge as shown.
- ✪ Place 12 stars in the corners of the blocks as shown and leave the 13th until the blocks are set.
- ✪ Using the dogtooth applique method described above, tuck the points under as you stitch.

- ✪ Remember the deeper the slashes the pointier your stars will be.

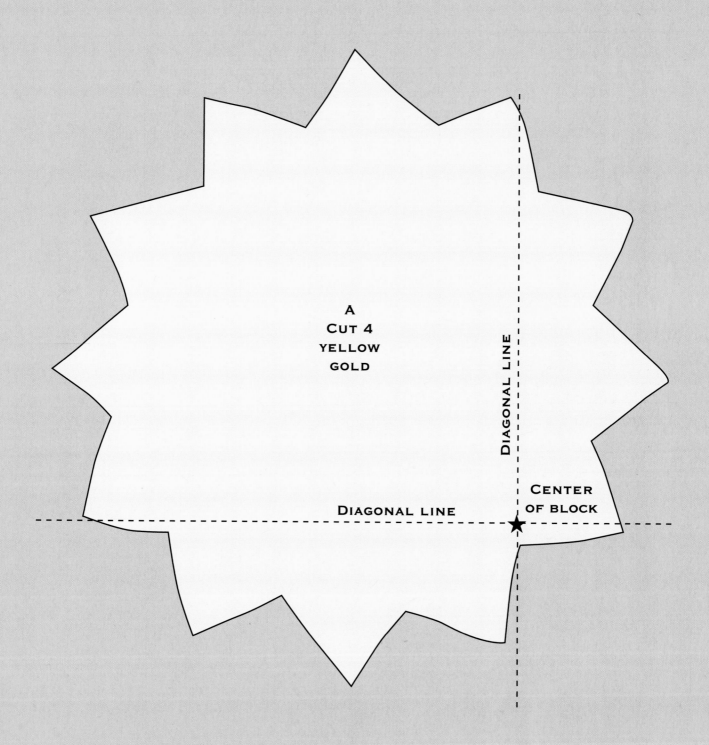

A
CUT 4
YELLOW
GOLD

DIAGONAL LINE

DIAGONAL LINE

CENTER
OF BLOCK

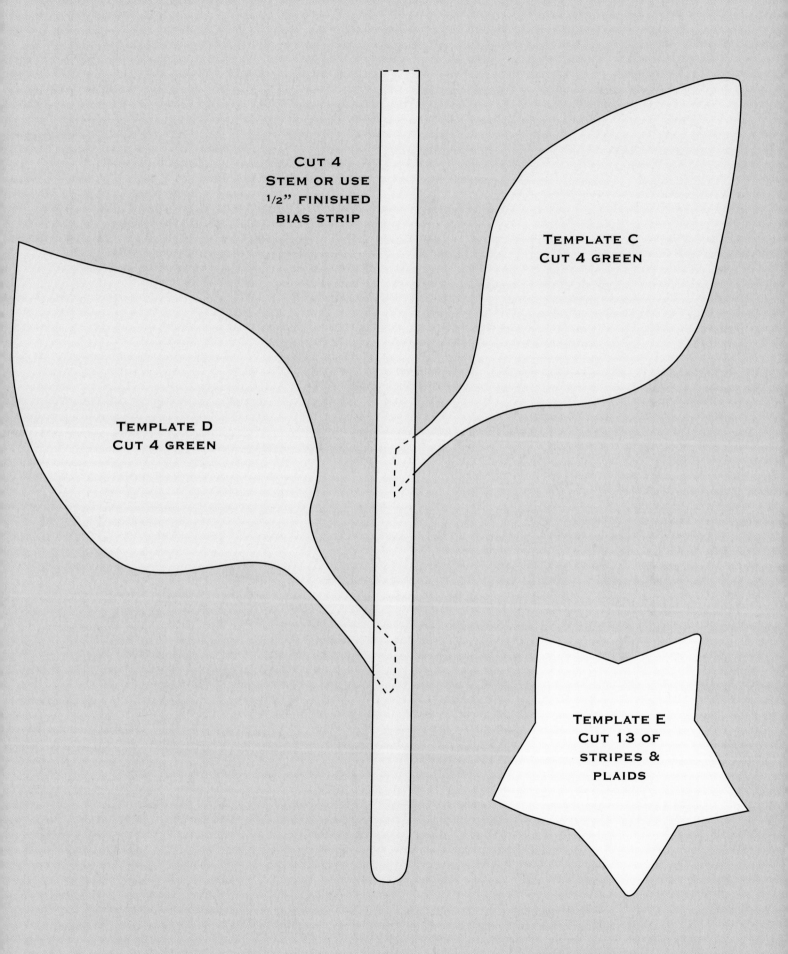

Cut 4
Stem or use
1/2" finished
bias strip

Template C
Cut 4 green

Template D
Cut 4 green

Template E
Cut 13 of
stripes &
plaids

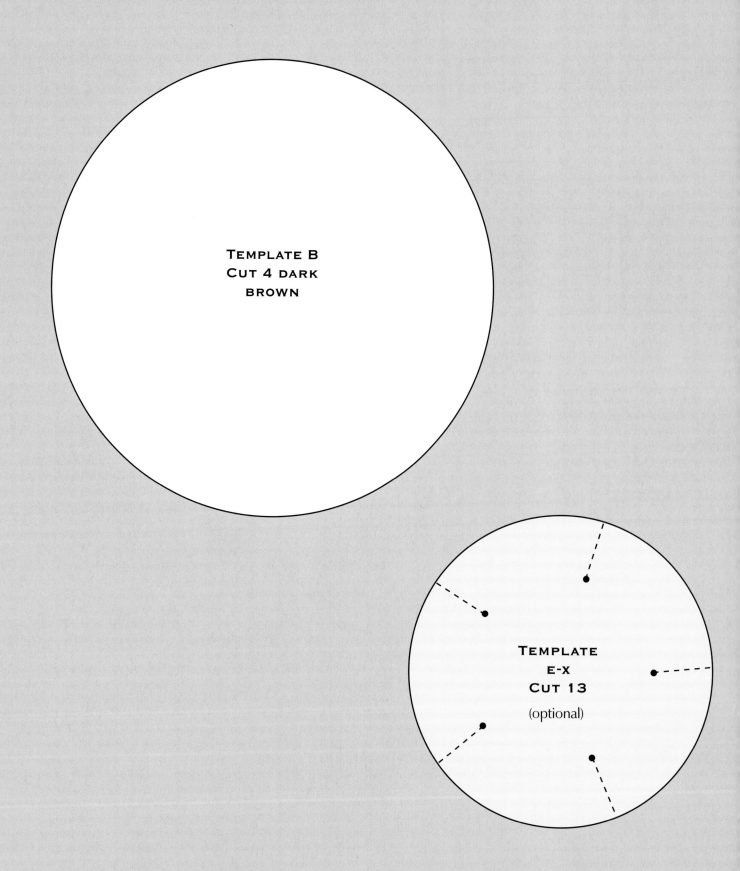

TEMPLATE B
CUT 4 DARK
BROWN

TEMPLATE
E-X
CUT 13
(optional)

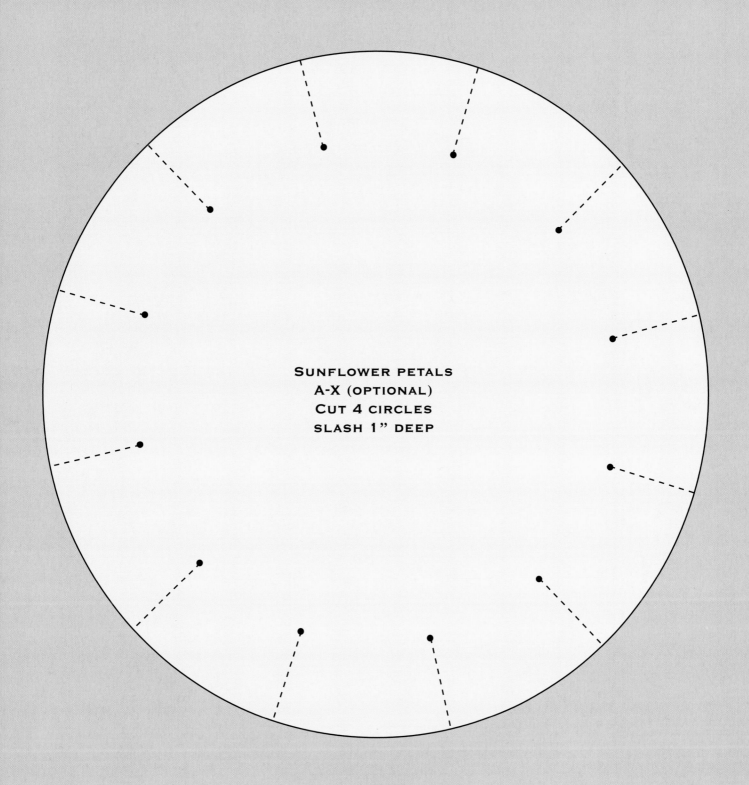

SUNFLOWER PETALS
A-X (OPTIONAL)
CUT 4 CIRCLES
SLASH 1" DEEP

BLOCK 10

ORDER NO. 11

FOR FANNIE KREEGER HALLAR
A CHILD IN WARTIME

14" Finished Block

The Order No. 11 Block was made by Jeanne Poore, Overland Park, Kansas.

DECADES AFTER THE Civil War, survivors wrote childhood memories of living through terrible times. One unusual reminiscence came in the form of a quilt pattern published in *The Kansas City Star* in 1929. Ruby Short McKim, *The Star's* quilt designer, described Fannie Kreeger Haller, a friend in Independence, as "a dear old lady in her eighties who was a little girl in Jackson County, Missouri, back in war times. [She] had seen her mother's choice new quilt snatched from the bed by marauders. She carried the memory of this striking pattern in her mind."

Fannie's name for the quilt pattern is obscure

to most today, but the words "Order Number 11" were code back then for all the injustices Missourians suffered during the Border Wars. After Quantrill's raiders burned the town of Lawrence, the U.S. Army directed that civilians living in Jackson, Bates, Cass and Vernon Counties "remove from their present places of residence within fifteen days." Order Number 11 was viewed by Kansans as a wise precaution to prevent more terrorism. Missourians saw it as a vicious act of revenge.

Artist George Caleb Bingham recalled the chaos as everyone left their homes.

Martial Law. An engraving by John Sartain after George Caleb Bingham's painting also called Order Number 11. In 1869 and 1870 Bingham painted two similar scenes of Union troops expelling Missouri citizens. He published this print about 1872. Illustration courtesy of the Library of Congress.

"Bare-footed and bare-headed women and children, stripped of every article of clothing except a scant covering for their bodies were exposed to the heat of August sun and compelled to struggle through dust on foot. All their means of transportation had been seized by their spoilers, except an occasional dilapidated cart or an old...horse."

George Washington Hallar was a frequent participant in the annual reunions of Quantrill's guerillas held around the turn of the century and reported in detail by the Kansas City Times, which had a soft spot in its editorial heart for the Lost Cause.

The Union troops also seized food and bedding, including Araminta Kreeger's new quilt. Martha Frances Kreeger (1853-1929) was ten years old when she became a refugee. She had seen a good deal of war by then. In her obituary, it was noted that the night before the Battle of Lone Jack, about a year earlier, she watched "General F. M. Cockrell with forces of Confederates camped in the pasture of her father's farm and [heard] the sound of the guns and the roar of the battle."

After leaving the Lone Jack farm in the late summer of 1863, the Kreegers walked east to either Carroll County or Lafayette. The *Lee's Summit Journal* published a vignette telling of their homecoming after the War. "When the George W. Kreeger family returned to their log home, they found it standing but the fences were gone and their hogs were wild. Mr. Kreeger built a rail pen and inveigled the hogs with food."

Fannie grew up to marry George Washington Hallar, known as Wash, who'd been a member of Quantrill's bushwhacker troops. They had a daughter Aileen who must have heard many memories of the Border Wars as she was growing up in the 1880s and '90s.

Order Number 11 is an old patchwork design going back to the 1830s with other names such as Hickory Leaf or the Reel. For another of Araminta Daniel Haller's quilts see the Seth Thomas Rose on page 90.

VISIT

The Lone Jack Battlefield Museum near Fannie Kreeger's childhood home. 301 South Bynum Road in Lone Jack.

The Lee's Summit Historic Cemetery has monuments to several well-known guerrilla fighters. Fannie's parents, George and Araminta Kreeger, are buried here as well.

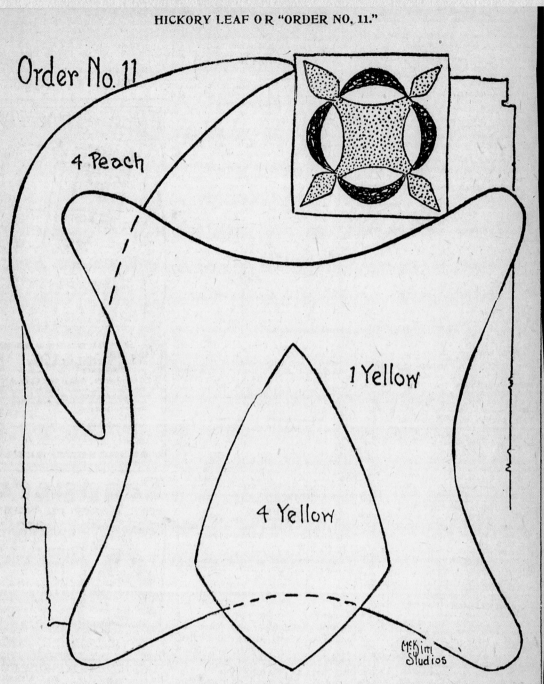

Order No. 11

4 Peach

1 Yellow

4 Yellow

McKim Studios

(Clip and Save.)

Quilt authorities may identify this pattern as the "Hickory Leaf," and it is doubtless of the stock of that pioneer favorite. But its story is this: Fannie Kreeger Haller, a 10-year-old girl, saw her mother's choice new quilt snatched from their bed by marauders back in 18— when Order No. 11 was the issue. She carried the treasured design in her mind and years after reproduced the quilt, christening it "Order No. 11," a local identification. A 12-inch square is the background onto which the nine curved sections applique. Patterns here given are the line to crease back to. So cut them all a seam larger.

(Copyright by The Kansas City Star, 1929.)

Order Number 11 appeared as an appliqué pattern in The Kansas City Star *in 1929. Ruby McKim spelled Martha Frances Kreeger's name Fannie Haller, but public records also show it as Fanny or Fannye Hallar.*

CUTTING DIRECTIONS

- ✪ Cut a light 15" square.
- ✪ Make a template for piece A, B and C. Do not add a seam allowance to the template Cut the amount of pieces needed as stated on each pattern piece..
- ✪ Draw around the template on the back of the fabric. Add 1/8" to 1/4" seam allowance to each piece as you cut it out.

TO MAKE THE BLOCK

- ✪ Fold the light 15" square in half vertically and horizontally. Press the creases in lightly. Refold the square from corner to corner twice and lightly press the creases in. The creases will help with the placement of the pieces.
- ✪ Appliqué 1 medium blue A piece to the center of the block. Line up the points of the piece with the creases that go from corner to corner. Stitch the four medium blue B pieces in place next. Add the dark C pieces last.
- ✪ Trim the square to 14 1/2" after you are finished with the appliqué work.

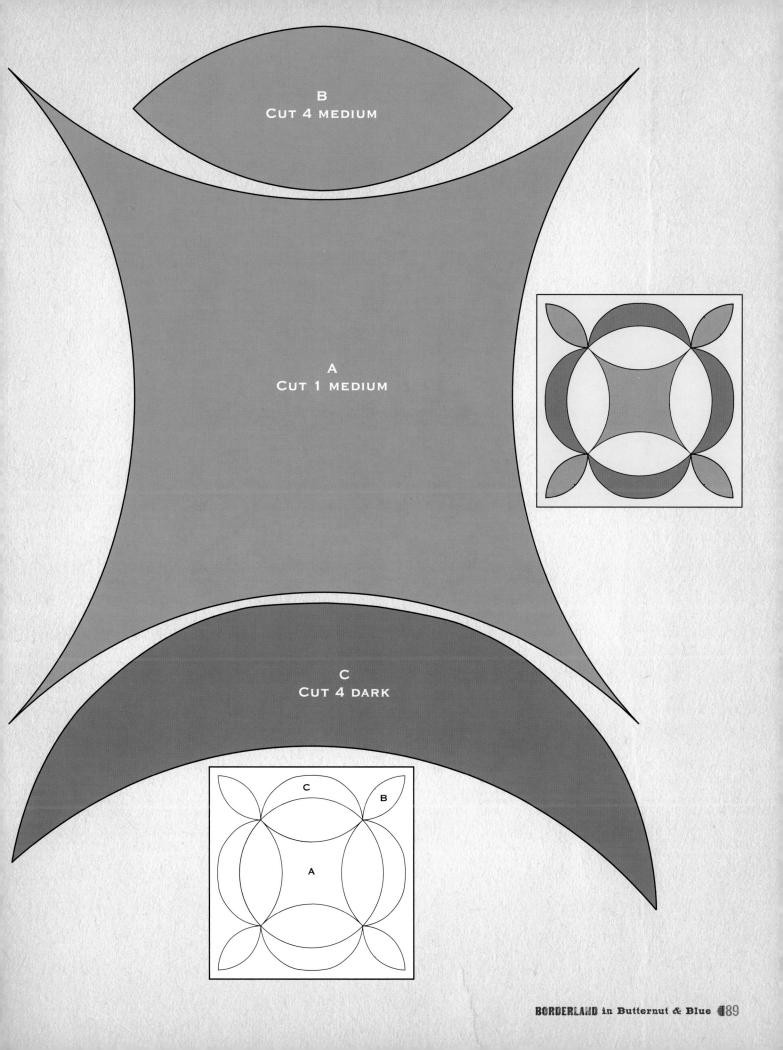

B
CUT 4 MEDIUM

A
CUT 1 MEDIUM

C
CUT 4 DARK

PROJECT 4
SETH THOMAS ROSE

28" square Quilt (one block)

Seth Thomas Rose, 28" square, hand appliquéd by Barbara Brackman, machine quilted by Pamela Mayfield, Lawrence, Kansas, 2007. A wall quilt to remember Araminta Daniel Kreeger and other victims of Order Number 11.

Fannie Hallar Must have loaned another of Araminta Kreeger's quilts to the *Star* pattern columnist. This one appeared as a pattern on October 12, 1929, telling readers that Araminta drew the pattern for a red and green quilt in 1862. Fannie, her eldest child, said she copied the design from the face of a Seth Thomas clock brought from North Carolina. Shelf clocks at the time often had glass doors with hand-painted scenes and florals.

Unlike her reel quilt, the rose quilt survived the Civil War. Perhaps she made it afterwards although one wonders when she got the time.

Frances Araminta Daniel Kreeger had twelve pregnancies between 1853 and 1875. She delivered two pairs of twins. Araminta died two days after her 45th birthday, a few weeks after the birth of her fourteenth child who only outlived her for a month.

She was born in North Carolina in 1830 and came to western Missouri with her family when she was young. She married George Kreeger when she was 22. He was a prosperous farmer when Order Number 11 forced them to leave the family farm with their six children, all under ten years of age.

Above: An unknown quilter made the Seth Thomas Rose design into a pillow cover, probably soon after the pattern appeared about 1930. Collection of Terry Clothier Thompson.

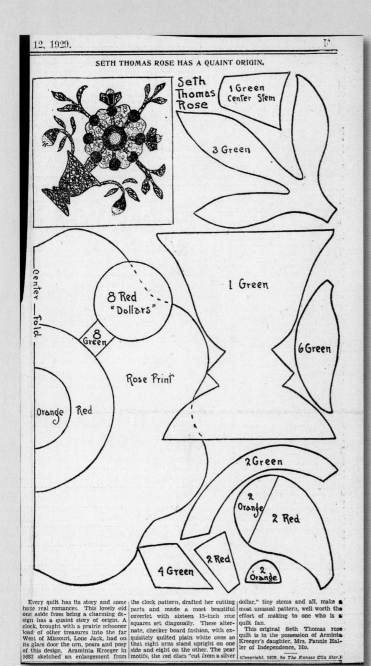

SETH THOMAS ROSE HAS A QUAINT ORIGIN.

Seth
Thomas
Rose

1 Green
Center Stem

3 Green

Center Fold

8 Red
"Dollars"

8 Green

Rose Print

Orange | Red

1 Green

6 Green

2 Green

2 Orange

2 Red

4 Green

2 Red

2 Orange

Every quilt has its story and some have real romances. This lovely old one aside from being a charming design has a quaint story of origin. A clock, brought with a prairie schooner load of other treasures into the far West of Missouri, Lone Jack, had on its glass door the urn, pears and posy of this design. Araminta Kreeger in 1862 sketched an enlargement from the clock pattern, drafted her cutting parts and made a most beautiful coverlet with sixteen 15-inch rose squares set diagonally. These alternate, checker board fashion, with exquisitely quilted plain white ones so that eight urns stand upright on one side and eight on the other. The pear motifs, the red discs "cut from a silver dollar," tiny stems and all, make a most unusual pattern, well worth the effort of making to one who is a quilt fan.

This original Seth Thomas rose quilt is in the possession of Araminta Kreeger's daughter, Mrs. Fannie Haller of Independence, Mo.

(Copyright, 1929, by The Kansas City Star.)

I enlarged the *Star's* 1929 pattern 120% to make a wall hanging of Araminta's Seth Thomas Rose and added a dogtooth appliqued border. The red circles are no longer the same size as a dollar.

Clocks like this one, manufactured by the Seth Thomas Clock Company of Connecticut, were decorated with popular images. Seth Thomas clocks were quite reliable but it might be that a few Yankee peddlers sold cheap counterfeits of "Connecticut wooden clocks", giving them the poor reputation with Missouri farmers.

"Every quilt has its story and some have real romances. This lovely old one aside from being a charming design has a quaint story of origin. A clock, brought with a prairie schooner load of other treasures into the far West of Missouri, Lone Jack, had on its glass door the urn, pears and posy of this design. Araminta Kreeger in 1862 sketched an enlargement from the clock pattern, drafted her cutting parts and made a most beautiful coverlet with sixteen 15" rose squares set diagonally. These alternate, checker board fashion, with exquisitely quilted plain white ones so that eight urns stand upright on one side and eight on the other. The pear motifs, the red discs 'cut from a silver dollar,' tiny stems and all, make a most unusual pattern, well worth the effort of making to one who is a quilt fan.
This original Seth Thomas rose quilt is in the possession of Araminta Kreeger's daughter, Mrs. Fannie Haller of Independence."

FABRIC

I used the palette described in the old newspaper pattern and reproduction prints echoing the colors popular for applique in the 1860s. I updated the look by using a print rather than plain background.

- ✪ 1 yard light print for background
- ✪ 1/2 yard Turkey red reproduction for border and applique
- ✪ Scraps of green, rose pink and cheddar yellow for applique
- ✪ Or buy a fat quarter each
- ✪ 1/4 yard across the width of the fabric of plain red for the binding

CUTTING

- ✪ Cut a 28" square from light fabric for the background.
- ✪ Cut the appliqué pieces using the templates, adding seam allowances of a scant quarter-inch.

BORDERS

- ✪ For the dogtooth border, cut 4 red strips 2" x 28 1/2" for the mitered borders.

SEWING THE BLOCK

- ✪ Fold and lightly press the background into quarters. Use the creases as a guide for appliqué placement.
- ✪ Prepare the appliqué pieces by turning the edges under and basting or gluing the seam allowances in place.
- ✪ Place the pieces as shown in the illustration and baste or glue them in place.
- ✪ Appliqué the pieces in place using your favorite method.

APPLIQUEING THE DOGTOOTH BORDER

- ✪ See pages 78 for information on stitching a dogtooth applique border. This border is similar to the one on the Sunflower quilt but the proportions are different and Barbara did not alter the corners to make them meet in regular fashion.
- ✪ Stay-stitch the red strip to the edge of the light background.
- ✪ Mark dots every 2" on the free edge of the red strip.
- ✪ Cut slits 1" long at each dot.
- ✪ Fold and applique each tooth.
- ✪ Miter the corners as you come to them.
- ✪ If you'd prefer a more regular corner, cut corner triangles of red fabric and
- ✪ add them over the edge of the corners. To cut these corners, cut 2 red 3 7/8" squares. Cut each one on the diagonal to make 2 triangles. Trim as necessary.

QUILTING

Pam Mayfield machine quilted the wall hanging using an old-fashioned style that echoed the appliqué in 1/4" waves. She put a 1" diagonal grid over the background and border.

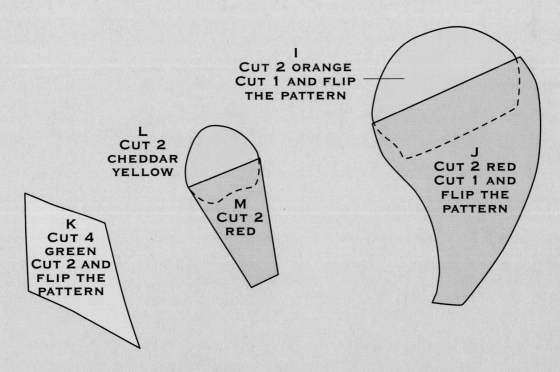

I
Cut 2 orange
Cut 1 and flip
the pattern

L
Cut 2
cheddar
yellow

M
Cut 2
red

J
Cut 2 red
Cut 1 and
flip the
pattern

K
Cut 4
green
Cut 2 and
flip the
pattern

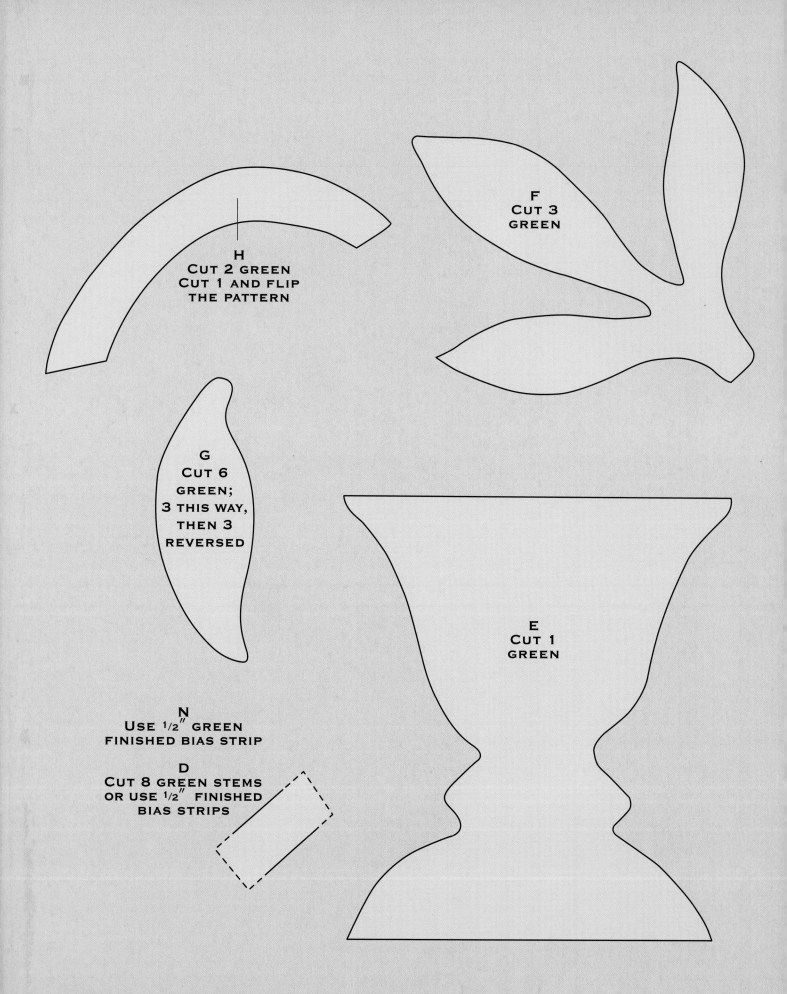

H
CUT 2 GREEN
CUT 1 AND FLIP
THE PATTERN

F
CUT 3
GREEN

G
CUT 6
GREEN;
3 THIS WAY,
THEN 3
REVERSED

E
CUT 1
GREEN

N
USE ½" GREEN
FINISHED BIAS STRIP

D
CUT 8 GREEN STEMS
OR USE ½" FINISHED
BIAS STRIPS

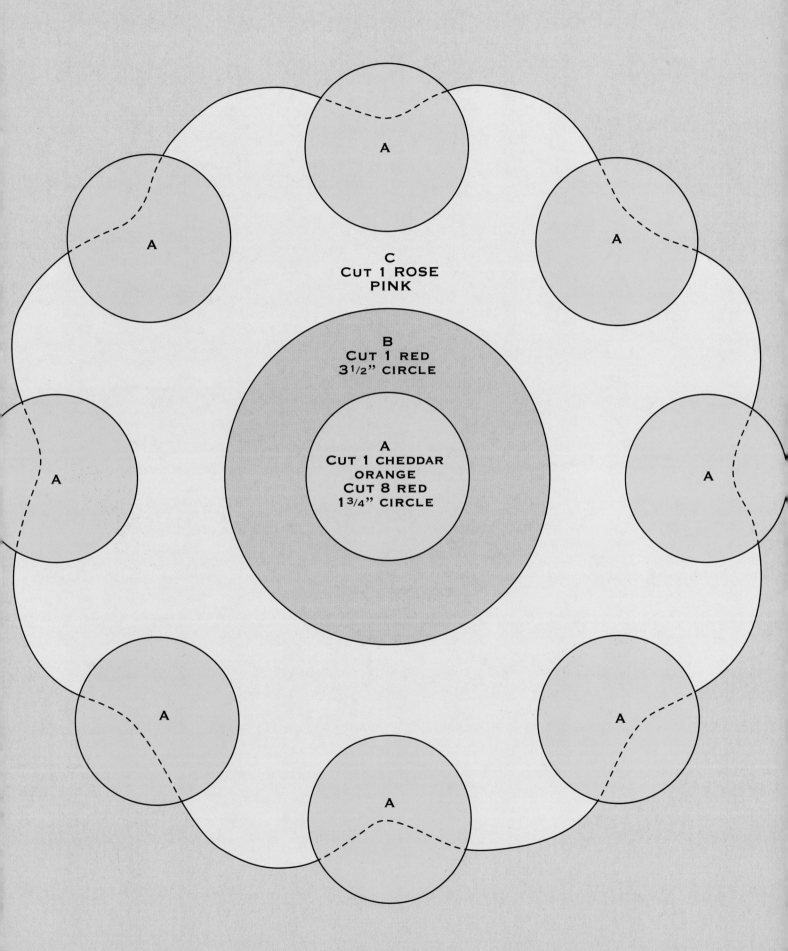

C
CUT 1 ROSE
PINK

B
CUT 1 RED
3½" CIRCLE

A
CUT 1 CHEDDAR
ORANGE
CUT 8 RED
1¾" CIRCLE

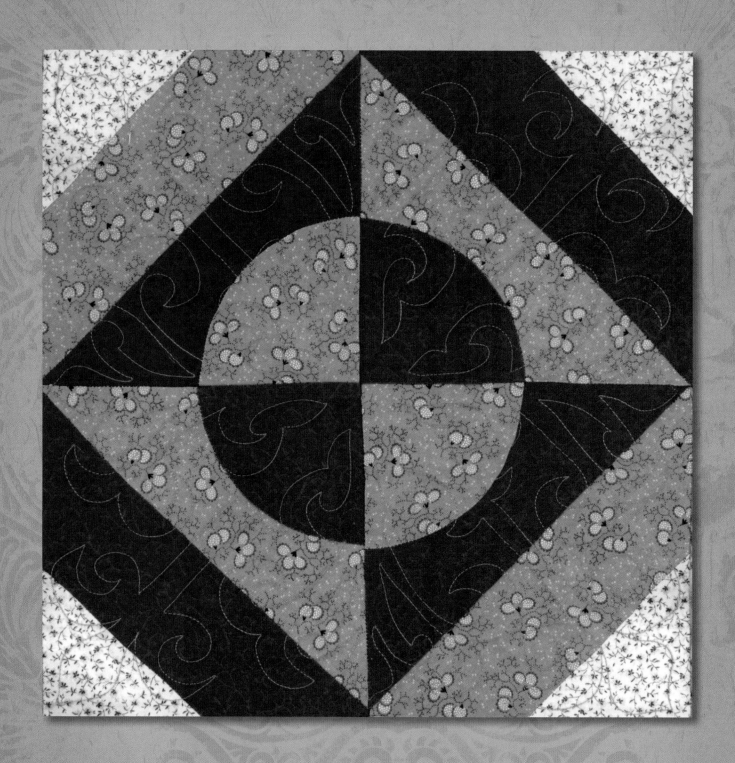

BLOCK II
SOUTHERN MOON
A BLOCK FOR MARGARET WATTS HAYS
AN OFFICER'S WIFE

14" Finished Block

THE SOUTHERN MOON BLOCK WAS MADE BY PAT MOORE, KANSAS CITY, KANSAS.

MARGARET WATTS WAS 16 in 1852 when she married Upton Hays, a great-grandson of Daniel Boone. Her husband freighted for the Santa Fe trading companies that operated out of the frontier town of Westport, Missouri, and was on the road for months in the summers of the 1850s. "It is a money making business & they have had very good luck so far!" she wrote her parents who had moved to California soon after the gold rush.

By 1856, Margaret wrote that Upton's activities in the proslavery militia caused them to worry about vengeful Kansans. "I do not think that Upton's life will ever be safe hear, in fact I know it." On a

lighter note: their young son John "calls himself the little Border Rufian."

Despite talk of Texas, the Hays stayed on their farm near what is now the corner of 63rd Street and Garfield. They kept a few slaves of their own plus those of Margaret's parents, people they would not take with them when they moved to the free state of California. Margaret's letters often contained news about the enslaved servants.

"Wilson is hired out to a widow woman across [the] Blue. Ned Noland bought Ben, Henery is grunting about all the time, he don't do anything

Above: Margaret Watts Hays about 1860. Photograph courtesy of Marian Franklin.

Elfleda and Mary Elizabeth Hays, about 1865. Photograph courtesy of Marian Franklin

much but [quarrel] and grumble. Sometimes he will lay up all week until Saturday then he will feel well enough to go to Westport. Nancy, she has been stouter this summer than she has been in the last three years. She is very anxious to be set free."

Margaret continued to write of hard times along the border. "The country has been full of excitement. Times get worse instead of better.... We have been overrun with Jayhawkers at Westport."

When the Civil War began, Upton, like many other Missouri Confederates, remained in Union Missouri. Viewing his duty as protecting his family, his neighbors and their property from Union troops and Kansas Jayhawkers, he fought in the Missouri ranks of the Confederate States of America. Popular with his men and bold in battle, he quickly rose to Colonel. Among his raids was a sack of the town of Gardner, Kansas, in October, 1861.

A month later Union troops were at the door. "I met [the Jayhawkers] on the portico and invited them in....I talked nicely to them and after a time they said they would not rob the inside but would take everything they could find outdoors....I am looking every hour for my house to be destroyed by these Jayhawkers."

Within a year Margaret had terrible news for her mother. "This evening of my birthday I received news of my husband's death. It has been published in the paper, but I do not believe it, as they have had him dead so often."

But the newspapers had it right; Colonel Hays was shot near the town of Newtonia, south of Joplin. Margaret, living with her brother-in-law's family, was left with an infant, three older children and little else. Her home had been burned by Jayhawkers and everything stolen. A new house that friends built for her was burned when she was forced to abandon it by Order Number 11.

A memorial to Upton Hays, Colonel in the army of the Confederate States of America, lies below the Confederate Monument at Forest Hill Calvary Cemetery on Troost. The Hays family spelled the name without an "e".

After the War, Margaret joined her parents in California. In 1877, she married William B. Overstreet, another veteran of the Border Wars who'd ridden with Quantrill. According to a descendent, "Every one knew that wasn't his real name." The 1900 census finds them living in Kings County, California, with their 22-year-old son Claude, a nephew and two granddaughters.

"[THE JAYHAWKERS] CAME TO OUR HOUSE, TOOK ALMOST 70 HEAD OF SHEEP AND 45 OR 50 HEAD OF THE FINEST STOCK THERE WAS IN THE COUNTRY. IN A FEW DAYS THEY CAME TO THE SAME HOUSE, TOOK THE NEGROES, WENT TO THE BEDS AND ROLLED THEM UP, SAYING THEY WOULD TAKE THEM TO THEIR WIVES." MARGARET HAYS, NOVEMBER 12, 1861.

Southern Moon is a block designed for the Laura Wheeler newspaper column in the early 1930s. The name calls to mind the full moon in the borderlands when the armies, regular and irregular, liked to ride.

TO READ MORE

About Margaret Hays and her family go online to a website featuring their remarkable collection of letters. www.wattshaysletters.com

VISIT

Kelly's Westport Inn on Westport Road at Pennsylvania. While you enjoy a beer at the bar, look out onto Westport Road and imagine the town of Westport. It was the major outfitting town on the Santa Fe Trail and this building, constructed in 1837, was its social center. The Boones opened their store in 1848.

The Ewing Boone Building in the early twentieth century. Photograph courtesy of the Westport Historical Society.

Kelly's Westport Inn now occupies the building where Upton Hays' Boone cousins and uncles maintained a store on the western trails in the 1840s and '50s.

ROTARY CUTTING

- ✪ A – Cut 2 light 4 3/8" squares. Cut each in half once on the diagonal to make 2 triangles.
- ✪ B – Cut 2 dark and 2 medium strips 3" x 11 1/2". Cut the angles using the template.
- ✪ C – Cut 2 dark and 2 medium strips 3" x 11 1/2". Cut the angles and curves using the template.
- ✪ D – Use the template to cut 2 dark and 2 medium pieces.

TO MAKE THE BLOCK

- ✪ Piece the block together in quarters.
- ✪ Stitch a medium C piece to a dark D piece.

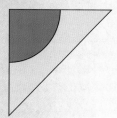

- ✪ Add a dark B piece then finish the section by adding the light A piece. Make two sections like this.

- ✪ Sew a medium D piece to a dark C piece.

- ✪ Add a medium B piece then finish the section by adding a light A piece. Make two of these sections.

- ✪ Sew the four sections together to complete the block.

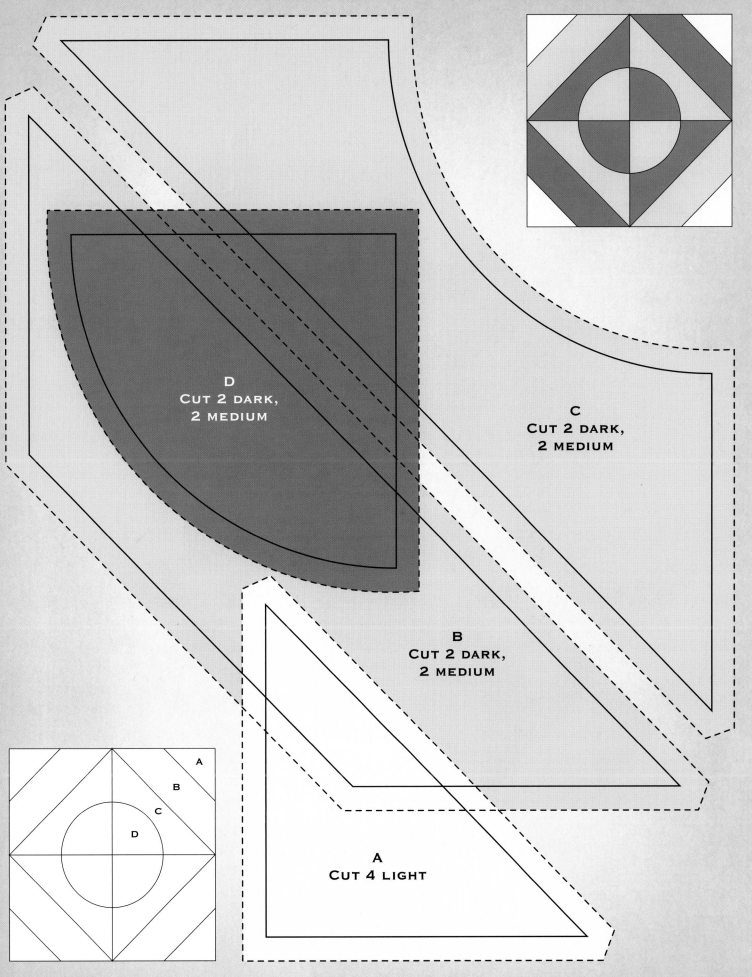

D
CUT 2 DARK,
2 MEDIUM

C
CUT 2 DARK,
2 MEDIUM

B
CUT 2 DARK,
2 MEDIUM

A
CUT 4 LIGHT

A
B
C
D

BLOCK 12

MISSOURI PUZZLE

FOR SUE MUNDY
A SOLDIER

14" Finished Block

THE MISSOURI PUZZLE BLOCK WAS MADE BY JEANNE POORE, OVERLAND PARK, KANSAS.

THIS NINE-PATCH IS perfect to recall Sue Mundy who is indeed a Missouri Puzzle. Many conflicting stories tell us who she was. Most describe a young Kentucky man named Marcellus Jerome Clarke who rode with Quantrill after the raid in Lawrence. He was tall yet delicate and some suspected he was actually a woman dressed in men's clothing. The newspapers printed sensational stories about the guerrilla exploits of Clarke's alter ego "Sue Mundy."

There are documented tales of women who did dress as men and fight in the Civil War but Clarke was a man, reliable information gathered after he was captured and hung as a guerrilla in 1865. Other tales tell of another Sue Mundy---a man who dressed as a woman to flirt and spy in Missouri and Kentucky. Several guerrillas might have used the name Sue Mundy, as "she" seems to have traveled throughout the Border States.

A real woman named Sue Mundy was arrested for aiding the guerrillas. She was one of the girls injured in the Kansas City jail collapse in August, 1863. She survived the war to marry Michael N. Womacks in 1873 and live out her life in Blue Springs. Did her name come to stand for female spies in the outrage that followed the jail collapse?

Sue Munday is one of the mysteries of the Border Wars. Was Sue a woman dressing as a man; a man dressing as a woman, or just good copy for the newspapers of the time? The pattern was printed about 1910 by Clara Stone, a New Englander who sold quilt designs. A similar pattern was printed in *The Kansas City Star* in 1930.

Above: Marcellus Jerome Clarke, a guerrilla fighter hung in 1865.

ROTARY CUTTING

- ✪ A - Cut squares 3 1/8". Cut each once on the diagonal to make 2 triangles.
  - ★ Cut 6 dark squares to make 12 triangles.
  - ★ Cut 6 light squares to make 12 triangles.
- ✪ B – Cut 4 light 5 1/2" x 2 3/4" rectangles.
- ✪ C – Cut 5 1/2" x 1 1/4" rectangles
  - ★ Cut 8 medium and 4 dark.
- ✪ D – Cut 1 dark 5 1/2" square.
- ✪ E – Cut squares 1 1/4".
  - ★ Cut 20 dark and 16 medium.

TO MAKE THE BLOCK

- ✪ Make 12 half-square triangle units by sewing the light and dark A triangles together.

- ✪ Sew the dark and medium E squares together to make 4 nine-patch units. See the diagram below for color placement.

- ✪ Now sew a medium C strip to either side of a dark C strip. Make 4 of these.

- ✪ We'll sew this block together in rows. There are 5 rows. Rows 1 and 5 are alike as are rows 2 and 4. Sew two half-square triangles together then add a B rectangle. Sew two more half-square triangles together to complete the row. Make two rows like this.

- ✪ Sew 1 half-square triangle to a nine-patch unit. Add a three-strip C unit, another nine-patch and finish the row with a half-square triangle. Make two rows.

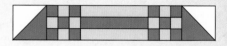

- ✪ Sew a light B rectangle to a three-strip C unit. Now add the dark D square. Sew on a three-strip C unit next and add a light B rectangle to complete the row.

- ✪ Sew the rows together to complete the block.

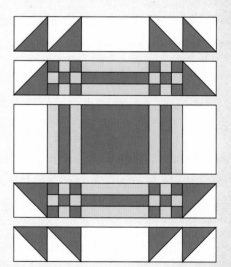

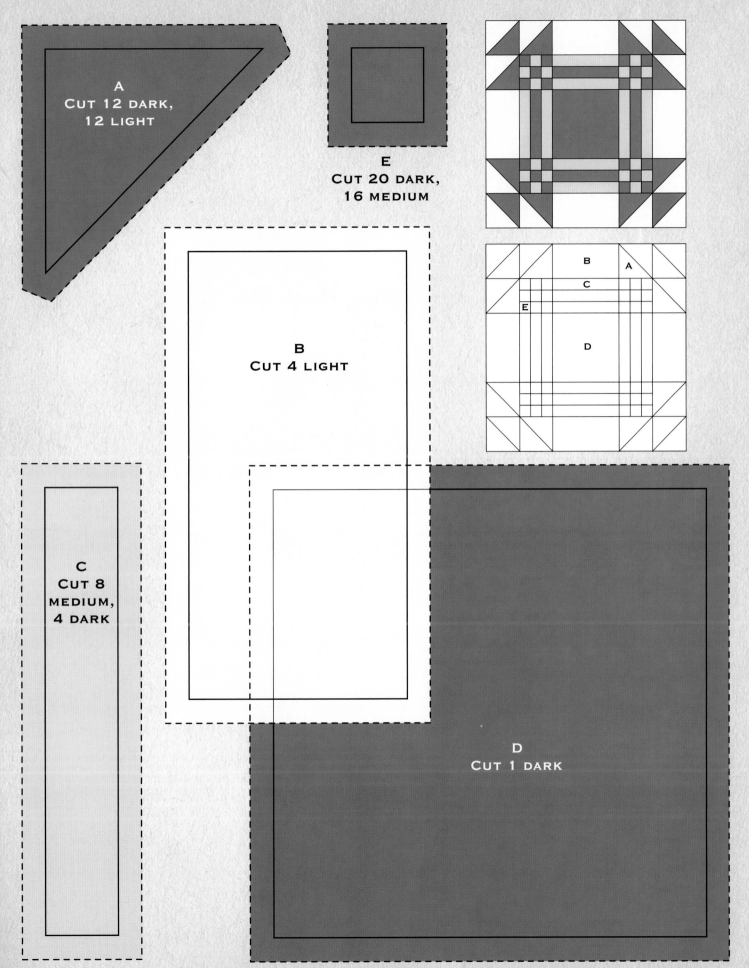

A
Cut 12 dark,
12 light

E
Cut 20 dark,
16 medium

B
Cut 4 light

C
Cut 8
medium,
4 dark

D
Cut 1 dark

BLOCK 13
CROWN OF THORNS
FOR BURSHEBA FRISTOE YOUNGER A REFUGEE

14" Finished Block
THE CROWN OF THORNS BLOCK WAS MADE BY PAT MOORE, KANSAS CITY, KANSAS.

BURSHEBA YOUNGER'S FAMILY played a part in nearly every act of the border conflict. In 1855, when Missourians claimed land in the new Kansas Territory, her husband Henry, a prosperous trader in Harrisonville, hoped to make Kansas a slave state by starting a town called Louisiana just outside the Shawnee Reservation in Douglas County. Although Henry actually lived with Bursheba and their 14 children in Missouri, he was elected to the first Kansas Legislature, known as the Bogus Legislature by the Kansans it governed, where he helped write pro-slavery laws.

After free-state settlers gained political control of Kansas, Missourians abandoned their hopes of another slave state across the state line and Henry opened a Cass County general store in 1857. When Civil War was declared, he supported the state's Union government like many proslavery Missourians. But neutrality was as dangerous as partisanship and Henry was shot on the road near the Shawnee Mission in 1862. His murder was probably revenge, either for his early proslavery politics in Kansas or for his sons' reputations. Cole and Jim rode with the bushwhackers. Some suspect the boys became guerrillas because of their father's death. Others surmise he was killed as a lesson to other parents who allowed their boys to run wild.

Above: Bursheba Fristoe Younger. Photograph courtesy of the State Historical Society of Missouri.

The widowed Bursheba could find no peace. Her house was burned and she became a refugee, living with relatives whose homes in turn were also destroyed by the Union Army or the Kansas Jayhawkers. Cole and Jim were among Quantrill's raiders who burned the town of Lawrence, Kansas in 1863, an act avenged by the Union Army's Order Number 11 that created a no man's land in the counties along the Kansas border. Bursheba and her youngest children walked south to Texas, settling near Sherman.

Once the shooting war was over, Bursheba's boys refused to surrender. With a few other guerrillas who turned to crime, the Youngers became Missouri folk heroes. Their mother was periodically terrorized, even after the War, by lawmen looking for the gang. She returned to Cass County, Missouri, in 1870 and died soon after at the age of 54.

The Nancy Page quilt column, a syndicated newspaper feature of the 1930s, printed this pattern with a religious name that reminds us of earthly sufferings. To Bursheba Younger and many other women on both sides the Border War was truly a crown of thorns.

VISIT

The Lee's Summit Historical Cemetery, 291 Highway and East Langsford Rd. Bursheba is buried with several of her children including James, Robert and Cole.

Four of Bursheba Younger's fourteen children. Henrietta stands behind brothers James, Robert and Thomas Coleman who rode with the bushwhacker armies in their youth and as outlaws after the war. Bob died in prison in 1889; Jim committed suicide in 1902 and Cole lived to join a Wild West Show in the early twentieth century. Photograph courtesy of the Library of Congress.

Thomas Nast created a series of engravings for Harper's Weekly during the Civil War. This vignette from "The War in the West" was published in January 1863, as Missouri was becoming infamous for the guerrilla war being fought there.

ROTARY CUTTING

- ✪ Piece A – Cut 4 light squares 4".
- ✪ Piece B – Cut squares 2 5/8". Cut each once on the diagonal to make 2 triangles.
  - ★ Cut 4 light squares to make 8 triangles.
  - ★ Cut 4 medium squares to make 8 triangles.
- ✪ Piece C – Cut 2 light squares 4 3/4". Cut each on the diagonal twice to make 4 triangles.
- ✪ Piece D – Cut squares 4 3/8". Cut each once on the diagonal to make 2 triangles.
  - ★ Cut 4 dark squares to make 8 triangles.
  - ★ Cut 2 medium squares to make 4 triangles.
- ✪ Piece E – Cut 1 dark 5 1/2" square.

TO MAKE THE BLOCK

- ✪ Sew a medium B triangle to either side of a C triangle. Add a light B triangle to either side then sew a light C triangle to the unit.

- ✪ Now add a dark D triangle to either side. You need to make 4 units like this. We'll call these the BCD units for clarity.

- ✪ To make the center of the block, sew a light D triangle to the four sides of the dark E square.

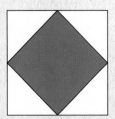

- ✪ Sew a BCD unit to either side to make the center strip.

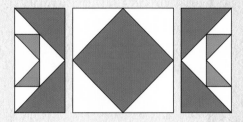

- ✪ Now sew a light A square to either side of a BCD unit. Make two strips like this, one for the top row and one for the bottom.

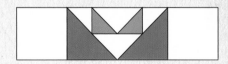

- ✪ Sew the three rows together to complete the block.

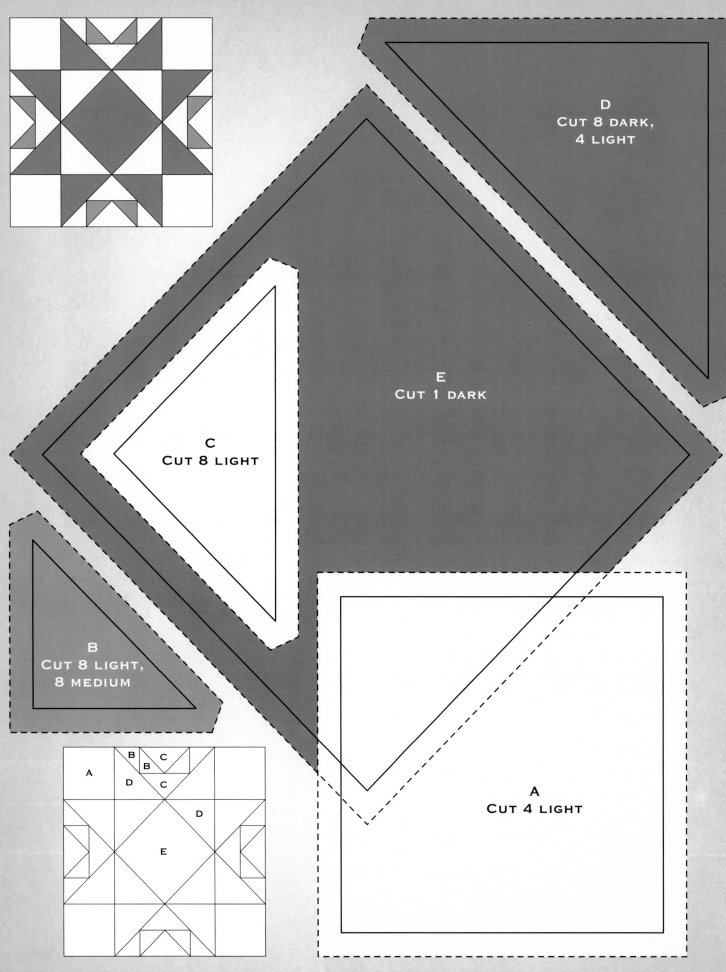

D
CUT 8 DARK,
4 LIGHT

E
CUT 1 DARK

C
CUT 8 LIGHT

B
CUT 8 LIGHT,
8 MEDIUM

A
CUT 4 LIGHT

PUTTING IT ALL TOGETHER

SETTING FOR THE 13 BLOCK SAMPLER

91" x 91"

Borderland Sampler made by Jeanne Poore, Overland Park, Kansas 2005.
Quilted by Fabrics Arts.

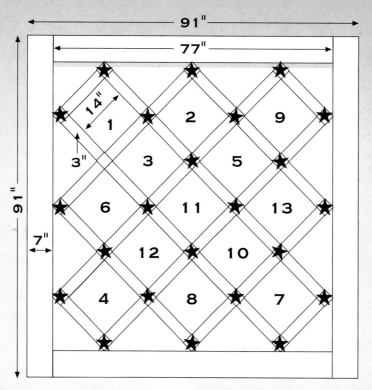

SETTING FOR THE 13 BLOCK SAMPLER

- ✪ 91" square
- ✪ 14" finished blocks
- ✪ 7" finished border
- ✪ 3" finished sashing

YOU NEED

- ✪ 13 blocks
- ✪ Sashing
- ✪ Cornerstones for the sashing
- ✪ Border
- ✪ Setting Triangles

FABRIC REQUIREMENTS FOR SET

- ✪ 4 1/2 yards blue for borders, sashing and bias binding
- ✪ 1/2 yard butternut for cornerstones
- ✪ 2 1/4 yards butternut for setting triangles. Use the same butternut for both and buy 2 3/4 yards.

CUTTING THE BORDERS

- ✪ Cut 2 strips 7 1/2" x 91 1/2" for the side borders
- ✪ Cut 2 strips 7 1/2" x 77 1/2" for the top and bottom borders.

CUTTING THE SETTING TRIANGLES

YOU NEED

- ✪ 8 side setting triangles
- ✪ 4 corner triangles
- ✪ Cut 2 squares 25 3/8". Cut each square twice on the diagonal. Make 8 side setting triangles.
- ✪ Cut 2 squares 15 1/8". Cut each square once on the diagonal to make 4 triangles for the corners.
- ✪ Cutting the Sashing and Cornerstones
- ✪ Cut 36 blue 3 1/2" x 14 1/2" strips
- ✪ Cut 24 butternut 3 1/2" squares

SETTING THE BLOCKS

- ✪ Sew sashing strips to the sides of the blocks as shown.
- ✪ Sew the blocks into strips on the diagonal as shown and add the side setting triangles and corner triangles to finish out each strip.
- ✪ Make long sashing strips by piecing cornerstones to strips as shown.
- ✪ Alternate these strips as shown.
- ✪ Add the last 2 corner triangles.
- ✪ Add the top and bottom borders.
- ✪ Add the side borders.

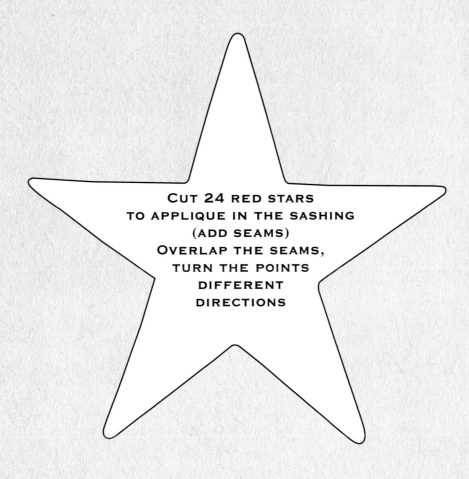

Cut 24 red stars
to applique in the sashing
(add seams)
Overlap the seams,
turn the points
different
directions

STARS ARE OPTIONAL, SEE
SHERRY DICUS' QUILT ON PAGE 2.

A STRIP SETTING FOR 12 BLOCKS

Quilt: 91 1/4" x 95"

Borderland Sampler made by Pat Moore, Kansas City, Kansas 2005.
Quilted by Kelly Ashton. Collection of Jacob Moore.

YARDAGE FOR THE STRIP SETTING

- ✪ 2 3/4 yards for triangles
- ✪ 6 yards for strips, border and binding

YOU'LL NEED:

- ✪ 12 Blocks finishing to 14"
- ✪ 48 triangles.
  - ★ Rotary cut 24 squares 10 7/8". Cut each square once on the diagonal to make 2 triangles.
- ✪ 4 Strips cut 8 ½" x 79 ½" for strips and side borders.
- ✪ 2 Strips cut 91 ¾ x 8 ½" for top and bottom borders.

SEWING

- ✪ 1. Sew a triangle to each side of a 14" block.
- ✪ 2. Make 3 strips of 4 blocks each.
- ✪ 3. Set the pieced strips between the 4 plain strips.
- ✪ 4. Add the top and bottom borders.

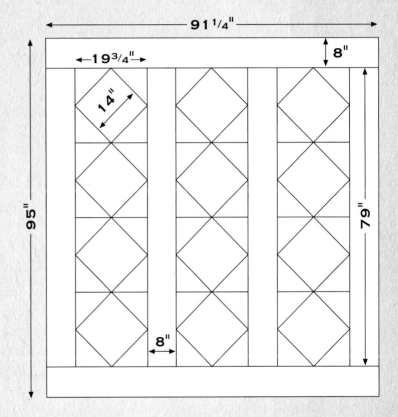

BUTTERNUT AND BLUE BY BETTY WEBER MCNEILL, OVERLAND PARK, KANSAS, 2004.
COLLECTION OF ANNA MCNEILL CALLAN.

BUTTERNUT AND BLUE BY D. JUNE FORD, OVERLAND PARK, KANSAS, 2004. QUILTED BY BETH
DAWSON. JUNE FRAMED TWELVE BLOCKS WITH NARROW TAN STRIPS, A TECHNIQUE THAT
ADDS VISUAL INTEREST AND ENSURES THAT THE BLOCKS CAN BE TRIMMED TO THE SAME SIZE.
THEY NOW FINISH TO 15". HER SASHING IS 3", THE INNER BORDER OF STRIPED FABRIC IS 6",
AS IS THE OUTER BORDER.

BUTTERNUT AND BLUE BY MAVIS MORRELL, KANSAS CITY, KANSAS, 2003-2004. QUILTED
BY WINDING RIVER QUILTING. MAVIS PHOTOCOPIED HER GREAT-GRANDFATHER LEWIS
WALKER'S 1865 DISCHARGE PAPERS FROM THE UNION ARMY ONTO FABRIC AND STITCHED THE
PRINT TO THE QUILT'S BACK.

BUTTERNUT AND BLUE BY ILYSE MOORE, 2005. OVERLAND PARK, KANSAS. 38" X 38". ILYSE REDRAFTED THE BLOCKS TO SIX INCHES AND ADDED A BORDER OF HER OWN DESIGN.

Rachel's Reel by Rita Briner, Lee's Summit, Missouri, 2006. Rita made this version of Order Number 11 from a pattern by Jo Morton that Jo calls Rachel's Reel.

BUTTERMILK AND BLUE, PIECED AND QUILTED BY DOROTHY LEBOEUF, ROGERS, ARKANSAS, 2005. DOROTHY COMBINED FIVE MEMORY WREATH DESIGNS WITH CORNER BLOCKS OF A SECOND PATTERN TO MAKE A QUILT SHE CALLS BUTTERMILK AND BLUE, A BRIGHTER PALETTE THAN THE TRADITIONAL BUTTERNUT AND NAVY. SET NINE OF THE 14" SAMPLER BLOCKS (NINE OF THE SAME IF YOU LIKE) USING THE ON POINT SETTING AND YOU'LL GET A BED QUILT 85 1/2" SQUARE.

SHOO FLY BY ELIZABETH ROBINSON SILER (1815-1879). POSSIBLY MADE IN BERKELEY
COUNTY, [WEST] VIRGINIA OR PLATTE COUNTY, MISSOURI. ESTIMATED DATE 1830-1850.
A FADED INK SIGNATURE ON THE BACK SAYS "ELIZ. SILER" AND A NOTE ATTACHED TO THE
QUILT READS, "QUILT MADE BY ELIZABETH SILER, GREAT GRANDMOTHER 146 YEARS AGO."
ELIZABETH AND PHILIP SILER CAME TO PLATTE COUNTY FROM THE WESTERN AREA OF
VIRGINIA IN 1846, BRINGING TWO YOUNG CHILDREN AND THIS QUILT. THE 1860 CENSUS
FOUND THEM IN WESTON KEEPING A BOARDING HOUSE.